**MO**

Other books by the same author:

Love that Heals (written jointly with Audrey)
Christian Prayer and Healing
Living in Victory (distributed privately)

# All You Need Is More and More of Jesus

Andy Arbuthnot

Highland
Guildford, Surrey

ISBN 0 946616 97 3

British Library Cataloguing-in-Publication Data.
A catalogue record for this book is available from
the British Library.



Published by Eagle, an imprint of Inter Publishing Service
(IPS) Ltd, 59 Woodbridge Road, Guildford, Surrey GU1 4RF



Typeset by Watermark, Crostwight Hall, Norfolk

Printed in Great Britain by HarperCollins, Glasgow

## DEDICATION

Although this book has been written by me, much of the inspiration has come from the encouragement and love of my wife, Audrey, and to her I gratefully dedicate this book. *A.A.*

All royalties from the sale of this book are being donated to the London Healing Mission.

# Introduction

This book has grown out of our work here at the London Healing Mission. My wife Audrey and I have worked here since April 1983, and during our time we must have counselled and prayed with many hundreds of individuals. So often, as we have seen them out of the front door, we have found ourselves saying to them, 'You will forget much of what we have said to you, but always remember that all you really need is more and more of Jesus.'

Most of the chapters in this book grew out of a short talk or sermon at one of the Healing Services we hold here several times a week. Many of them became letters and went out to all those on our mailing list. Some of them have come to be written up as articles for Christian magazines. Now they are gathered together in book form.

One of our team once said to me, 'I was brought up in the Brethren and there learned to know my Bible. We then moved to a Baptist church and I learned fellowship. We went to our present church and I found the Holy Spirit. I then joined you at the Mission and you showed me Jesus.'

*The London Healing Mission,*
*20 Dawson Place, London W2 4TJ*
*Tel: 071-229 3641*

# Contents

Introduction 7
1 The Power in the Name of Jesus 11
2 More and More of Jesus 14
3 Three Questions 17
4 How Do I Love Him? 21
5 On Loving God 26
6 God is More Important than His Work 31
7 Help! I've Gone Dry! 35
8 God Comes to Us in the Stillness 38
9 Difficulty with 'Love' 42
10 Faith 45
11 Praying in the Name of Jesus 48
12 What I Have, I Give 53
13 'Unless You Become Like Little Children' 58
14 On Accepting Jesus' Love 62
15 Power in Prayer 68
16 Why Does God Allow Suffering? 73

17 But Doesn't Prayer Work? 77
18 Robert Hasn't Been Healed 83
19 What Does Jesus Feel About Us? 89
20 On Loving Myself 94
21 On Touching Jesus 99
22 'I Can't Help Worrying' 104
23 Tolerance? Or Speak Out? 108
24 'L' Plates 113
25 Be Practical 118
26 Of Time and Eternity 124
27 The Humility of God 128
28 Listening in Prayer 131
29 Persist in Prayer 135
30 What Actually Happens at Holy Communion 139
31 God is Supernatural 143
32 The Exercise of Self-Discipline 147
33 Letting Go of Anger 152
34 Delayed Healings 157
35 Sins in Thought 162
36 The Sovereignty of God 166
37 Do I Have to Forgive? 172
38 What Really Happened on Calvary? 177
39 The Victory of the Cross 182
40 The Motorway 185

CHAPTER 1

# The Power in the Name of Jesus

During the spring of 1975 I gradually made a discovery. Up to then I had prayed to 'God' – and I knew that my prayer life was pretty deficient. I then began deliberately to address myself to 'Jesus'. My praying started to come alive. For the first time I was beginning to know the person I was praying to. I began to realise His love for me. I moved into an awareness of His gentleness and His compassion, and at the same time the sureness of His leading. My life began to unfold. Jesus said, 'Anyone who has seen me has seen the Father' (John 14:9).

This book is about Jesus. The early church knew about Jesus. Read the book of Acts again and you will see how often they used the name of Jesus. When the cripple called out to Peter and John asking for money, Peter replied, 'Silver or gold I do not have, but what I have I give you. In the name of Jesus Christ of Nazareth, walk' (Acts 3:6).

Many people pray to their 'heavenly Father' and in doing this they must be right. After all,

Jesus said, 'This, then, is how you should pray: "Our Father in heaven"' (Matthew 6:9). Yet somehow the power is in the name of Jesus.

One of the model prayers in the Bible was prayed by the early church when Peter and John were released after healing the cripple. The prayer begins, 'Sovereign Lord' (Acts 4:24). How descriptive those words are! 'Lord' in the original meant the fountain of all authority. In political terms the Roman empire was like an enormous pyramid. All power throughout the empire derived ultimately from one man at the top of the pyramid. He was Caesar and his title was 'Lord'. When the early church prayed to God as 'Sovereign Lord' they were using the word 'Lord' in the sense of the ultimate and absolute authority. To address Him in addition as 'Sovereign' reinforced their acceptance of God as being supreme.

Yet the words at the end of that prayer speak so strongly to us: 'Stretch out your hand to heal and perform miraculous signs and wonders through the name of your holy servant Jesus' (Acts 4:30).

It seems clear from what Jesus Himself said that He recognised the power that had been given to Him. Minutes before His final ascension into heaven He declared to His remaining disciples, 'All authority in heaven and on earth has been given to me' (Matthew 28:18). I used to ask myself who could ever have been in a position to give anything extra to Jesus – crucified, buried, resurrected and now about to ascend to heaven. There was only one person who could have given that authority to Jesus, and that was God the Father.

In Old Testament times the Jews knew the personal name of God. They had no vowels in their writing and we have tried to reconstruct the name as either Yahweh or Jehovah. After around 400 BC the Jews never spoke God's name – not even the high priest did. They were so aware of the power in the name that they simply didn't dare to speak it out aloud. God's personal name was finally lost.

I remember for a time praying earnestly, 'Lord, we need your power so desperately today. Don't you think it would be a good idea if you revealed your personal name to your people once again?' Then I realised that there was no need for God to reveal His name again. He had already put all authority into the name of Jesus.

We have learned more practical theology from coming up against the sheer power of evil in the spiritual warfare than we have from any theological treatise. When one is confronting evil, it is no use invoking the name of 'God'. It is no good commanding unclean spirits to go in the name of 'Christ' – Christ is only a word meaning the same as the Hebrew 'Messiah', that is, 'Anointed'. We know full well from experience in confronting the powers of darkness that we dismiss them in the name of 'Jesus'.

Thus it is that most formal prayers in use today are addressed to God the Father, but end with the words, 'through Jesus Christ our Lord'. The tragedy is that too often people have forgotten the power in the name of Jesus.

CHAPTER 2

# More and More of Jesus

In Jesus' day advanced thinkers in Jerusalem were realising the impossibility of keeping all the rules and regulations which had been handed down to them. They were wrestling with this question: 'There must be some basic law which undergirds all the law and the prophets. Which is it?'

Jesus must have had this question put to Him many times during the course of His earthly ministry, and from the record in the Gospels we find that He always gave the same answer. On one occasion a teacher of the law asked Him outright: 'Of all the commandments, which is the most important?' (Mark 12:28).

Jesus picked out two verses from Deuteronomy 6 and Leviticus 19 in His reply:

> 'The most important one ... is this: "... Love the Lord your God with all your heart and with all your soul and with all your mind and with all your strength." The second is this: "Love your neighbour as yourself." There is no commandment greater than these' (Mark 12:29–31).

If we are talking to one of our neighbours, perhaps in the queue at the checkout of the local supermarket, it doesn't come naturally to us to talk about 'the first and greatest commandment'. In everyday language we would say 'the most important thing in life'. Jesus is saying that the most important thing in life is meant to be our relationship of love with God.

God revealed Himself in the person of Jesus. Jesus said, 'I am in the Father, and ... the Father is in me' (John 14:10). He said, 'No-one comes to the Father except through me' (John 14:6). He said He could only do what He saw the Father doing (John 5:19). One of the main themes of John's Gospel is Jesus' total identification of Himself with His Father in heaven. John sums it up in the words, 'He who has Christ, God's Son, has God the Father also' (1 John 2:23, Living Bible).

If this relationship of love is the most important thing in my life, then it follows that it is also meant to be the most important thing in the life of anyone who comes to me for ministry. Therefore whatever the problem they come with, I always go first for their personal relationship of love with Him. If we can help a person into a fuller and more wonderful relationship of love with Him, we know that therein lies the healing and the wholeness for which the Lord in His love longs, for each of us.

Naturally when a person comes to us we will also give due attention to whatever their presenting problem may be. Indeed, in the course of a normal appointment here at the London Healing Mission, one can do quite a lot of talking in the space of the ninety minutes which we give people.

But as I see a person out of the door after their appointment, that is the moment to come back to fundamentals. So often I find myself saying, 'I don't really mind if you forget everything I have been saying to you, provided you remember one thing. It is as true for you as it is for me. It is this: All you need is more and more of Jesus.'

Where does God come in? For the answer we turn to 1 Corinthians 15:24–28. 'Then the end will come, when [Jesus] hands over the kingdom to God the Father ... then the Son himself will be made subject to him ... so that God may be all in all.'

I don't believe we can go further than this as we try and understand something of the heavenly relationship that exists between God the Father and God the Son.

Perhaps we can see something of that relationship when we look at the relationship in this country between the constitutional monarch and the Prime Minister. In years gone by the monarch had absolute authority. But more and more that authority was transferred to the Prime Minister. Today the monarch, although the titular head (and technically the source of all power), has personally retained little real power. Perhaps this reflects something of the present relationship between God the Father and God the Son where the battle against Satan is concerned: Jesus has been given all power until He finally emerges as victorious in every sphere. Then indeed He will hand over everything to the Father, and God will be 'all in all'.

CHAPTER 3

# Three Questions

When people I haven't met before ask me to pray for them, I always start by asking three questions. 'Does Jesus love you? Do you love Him? Have you given your life to Him?'

We learn so much from the answer to the first question. Sometimes the reply will come back without hesitation, as the smile broadens into a grin: 'Yes, of course He loves me!' At other times the person will be thoughtful and then say: 'Well, I hope He does.' One of the biggest problems in ministry is helping people to accept that they really are loved by Jesus.

Sometimes we ask them whether they are worthy of His love. The answer to that question is a resounding 'No!' None of us can possibly deserve to be loved by Him. Jesus is enthroned on high, the Son of the living God, perfect man and perfect God; what right could any of us possibly have to expect Him to come down to our level and actually love us as we are?

But He does.

There is only one reason why He loves us. It is not because we deserve His love. It is simply because He is made that way. As John wrote:

'God is love' (1 John 4:8). He can't help loving us, because it is His nature to love. Because He is perfect He is always true to His own nature.

If we can't (or won't?) take in that He loves us, it is we who are rejecting Him. 'Surely you wouldn't want Jesus to suffer the pain of rejection at your hands?' we often ask. It is a fact that, in loving us, He makes Himself vulnerable to us, and it's worth pondering the fact that we can actually hurt Him, the Son of God, by failing to accept His love for us. That amounts to our rejecting Him.

'Do you love Him?' we then ask. I remember the man who said: 'I'm not going to deceive you. I'm not going to be hypocritical, and the only truthful answer I can give to your question is that I don't love Him.' I respected that man, but he was mistaken in his understanding of love. He wanted to love Jesus, but he didn't know how to.

St John makes it clear in his writings that loving Jesus means obeying Him. He quotes Jesus' own words: 'If you love me, you will obey what I command' (John 14:15). John repeats this theme in his first letter: 'This is love for God: to obey his commands' (1 John 5:3).

We can't necessarily control our feelings, but we have a will which can say (if we want to): 'Yes, I am going to obey Jesus.' If we say that and we carry it through to the best of our ability, then, as St John makes clear, we are in fact loving Him. Moreover, if we do that, in time the very feelings of loving Him will grow in us. Thereafter, we won't have any doubt about whether we love Him or not!

My third question is: 'Have you surrendered

your life to Him?' There is a theme which runs right through the Bible which says, in effect, 'If you want My help, you must do it My way.' As we reflect, the reason is obvious: God designed us, created us, and brought us into being, and it must therefore follow that if we are really to come alive in the way God intended, we must follow God's directions. Part of His instruction to us is that we must surrender ourselves to Him completely. If we don't do that, and if we hold back in this area or that, we are actually putting up barriers and thereby preventing Him from working fully in us.

I always ask these three questions regardless of what a person's presenting problems may be. My reason is that the three questions all revolve around our relationship of love with Him. Jesus said that this was the most important thing in our lives and if that be the case, then it must be the most important thing – or is meant to be the most important thing – in the life of the person we are trying to help.

There may be many reasons why people find it hard to accept the love of Jesus for them. Sometimes it is unbelief. It may be sin which has not been faced up to. Very often it is their bad experience in human relationships, usually with their parents. This is where our ministry comes in. If we can help them to accept Jesus' love for them, as they are, then they are half way to loving Him themselves. John wrote, 'We love because he first loved us' (1 John 4:19).

Then, once the relationship of love has been established, it follows naturally that we want to give ourselves totally to Him in love and obedience. I believe that all real healing originates in that dynamic relationship of love between Him and us.

Many excellent books have been written on Christian counselling, but I believe the root of all Christian counselling is, under the Holy Spirit, to help the person for whom we are praying to enter, or to enter more deeply, into this relationship of love with his or her Lord and Saviour.

There is such wonderful security, and indeed safety, for us, when we realise that however good we may strive to be, we can't induce Him to love us more than He does already. Similarly, however bad we are He won't love us any less. He loves us with a love which is, quite simply, perfect love.

CHAPTER 4

# How Do I Love Him?

The Greeks realised 2000 years ago that anything is at its best when it is free to do what it was created to do. A fish is at its best when it is free to swim in the water. A bird is at its best when it is free to fly through the air. The same is true of the human being. We are at our best when free to do what we were designed to do.

Quite simply, the human being was designed and created for the express purpose of worshipping God, who revealed Himself in Jesus. This is why Jesus gave us what He called 'the first and greatest commandment'. Our whole life, He said, is to revolve around our relationship of love with the Lord. God refers to 'my people, my chosen, the people I formed for myself that they may proclaim my praise' (Isaiah 43:20–21).

There is a fundamental difference between the commandment to love the Lord and the second of His great commandments. The second commandment tells us to love our neighbours as ourselves. Jesus was pointing in that second commandment to a mutual flow of love between our neighbours and ourselves. It used to puzzle me that, as expressed in the first of these two commandments, the flow of love seems to be one way, that is from us to God. But of course Jesus was taking God's love for us for granted. I believe God's promise to love us is the only unconditional promise in the Bible. Paul wrote:

> 'I am convinced that neither death nor life, neither angels nor demons, neither the present nor the future, nor any powers, neither height nor depth, nor anything else in all creation, will be able to separate us from the love of God that is in Christ Jesus our Lord' (Romans 8:38–39).

When we express our love for God, we are not setting up a one-way flow of love from us to Him. Rather we are completing the two-way flow of love, since God is already loving us. Thus we see that each of the two commandments in which Jesus summarised all the Old Testament teaching envisages a mutual or two-way flow of love, on the one hand between the Lord and ourselves, and on the other between our neighbour and ourselves.

Loving God starts with the decision to love Him. Love finds its fullest expression in worshipping Him. As we worship Him we pour out our hearts before Him, in an ecstasy of joyful surrender to Him.

But how do we do this? For many people prayer is a mechanical exercise and too often devoid of feeling. Moreover if we look for 'feelings' in prayer we certainly won't find them, because then we are looking for feelings rather than looking for the reality of Jesus.

I find it can help in prayer to choose a passage

from one of the Gospels, to read it aloud a couple of times and then recount the story one has read, in one's own words, to an imaginary stranger. Let me give you an example.

Bartimaeus was a blind beggar sitting on the roadside just outside Jericho (Mark 10:46). People say that he had his blind man's cloak in the same way that today a blind person will have a white stick. It can't have been much of an existence for him. The heat in Jericho below sea level is intense and he would have depended for his existence on passers-by throwing the occasional coin in his direction.

You can picture the road, which would have been no more than a sandy track where the grass had been worn away by the feet of men and animals as they passed to and fro, either entering Jericho or setting out on the long climb up to Jerusalem.

Goats would have wandered across the track as they sought to graze wherever there was a patch of grass. Chickens would have been scratching in the dust under the old olive trees which stood with their gnarled trunks on either side of the track.

Here Jesus was walking with His disciples and a group of hangers-on. Bartimaeus must have learned from local gossip that the young prophet from Galilee was in the neighbourhood, and when he heard the group of people passing by he called out. We don't know if he was born blind but how he must have longed to be able to see. How he must have longed to be able to move around independently instead of relying on folk to lead him. Being able to see would mean independence and being able to lead a normal life. So it was with desperation that he shouted out, 'Jesus, Son of David, have mercy on me!'

To begin with, he got nothing for his pains other than perhaps a kick in the ribs from one or other of the passers-by, as they growled at him to shut up and stop distracting them from this young prophet with whom they were walking. But this made Bartimaeus cry out all the more.

Then Jesus heard him and stopped. 'Call him,' he said. We can imagine some of those in the group calling to Bartimaeus, 'You are in luck today! The prophet is asking for you. Up you get, He wants to say something to you.'

Bartimaeus threw away his blind man's cloak – that in itself was an expression of his faith in Jesus' ability to heal him.

Then Jesus put to him what seems at first to have been an unnecessary question. 'What do you want me to do for you?'

But so often Jesus seemed to provoke people to reach out and claim positively the healing they looked for.

Bartimaeus responded, saying with a shout that he wanted to see!

Jesus healed him. There would have been a moment of stunned silence as Bartimaeus realised that, possibly for the first time in his life, he could see clearly. At first the crowd who had gathered round did not take in what had happened. Then excitement broke out. Bartimaeus could see, and the crowd realised it, and they were pressing round Jesus, expressing their thrill at seeing Jesus' miracle and shouting with delight. Perhaps Bartimaeus had never seen his wife or his children. Now he would be able to see them. Now he would be able to find his way to his own home unaided. Now he would be able to lead a normal life. What joy there must have been in his heart! And how that joy must have been shared by that cheering crowd around him!

All eyes were on Jesus. I don't believe that they actually went up to Jesus and patted him on the back, saying, 'Well done, Rabbi.' Jesus had an air of authority about Him and people were accustomed to treating Him with respect. But there would have been a real sense in which the people were worshipping Jesus by the way they were admiring Him, respecting Him, thanking Him and in a very real way loving Him for what He had done.

I believe that if we look at the expression on Jesus' face there would have been a quiet smile and a radiance as He realised once again that He had fulfilled the purpose for which He came into this world, namely to rescue people from the darkness of Satan's kingdom.

Try it yourself. Take one of the stories of Jesus and, as you tell it to your imaginary friend in your own words, filling in the details which the Bible omits, something of the excitement of the crowd will communicate itself to you. You too will be saying to Jesus, 'Jesus, I want to love You. I love You and I join with the crowd in worshipping You in love and admiration.'

Human beings were created to love the God we see revealed in Jesus. As we love Him, we worship Him.

CHAPTER 5

# On Loving God

The story is told of a vicar who went to a new parish. There was a good turn-out on his first Sunday because everyone wanted to know if the new vicar could preach. They weren't disappointed! He preached a really good sermon on loving God. After the service they all went home and rang their friends, saying, 'We've got a really good vicar and he's a good preacher!' The next Sunday the church was fuller than ever and, as the vicar mounted the steps to the pulpit, the congregation were sitting forward on the edge of their seats, eagerly waiting to hear what he was going to preach about this Sunday. They couldn't quite make out what was happening when he then preached exactly the same sermon.

'He must be a bit absent-minded,' they said to each other as they left the church. 'Perhaps he forgot that he preached that sermon last Sunday. Anyhow, let's be sure we go again next Sunday to hear what he's going to preach about then.'

The next Sunday came. The members of the congregation were once again holding their breath to see what he was going to preach about.

As his sermon unfolded they realised that he was preaching exactly the same sermon once again.

After the service one of the churchwardens took the vicar aside. 'Vicar,' he said, 'that was a very good sermon, but you will be preaching a different sermon next Sunday, won't you?'

'No,' the vicar replied. 'I am going to go on preaching to them about loving God until they actually do it.'

I cannot guarantee that that story is true! It does, however, seem to me to be self-evident that if Jesus Himself said that the first and greatest commandment is to love God with all our heart, with all our soul, with all our mind and with all our strength, then we should take that seriously.

The very word 'commandment' can be misleading. In our daily lives we are not accustomed to being given 'commandments' to keep. Often, however, we are aware of having certain rules which we are to keep – at school, for instance, or later on when we are in employment. In many ways the force of what Jesus was saying comes across better if we change the wording slightly so that we hear Him saying that the most important rule in life is to love God with everything we've got.

But many people will then ask: 'How do I love God?' It is not easy to love someone you cannot see or feel, and cannot normally hear. How do we start on this business of loving Him?

I think there are five parallels which we can draw from marriage. As we look at them, we will see five ways in which we can be helped to love the God who revealed Himself in Jesus and with whom Jesus identified Himself so completely.

When boy meets girl, long before there is any question of marriage, they start to get to know each other. Usually there is no question of their loving each other until they get to know each other. We cannot really love the Lord until we begin to get to know Him. We need to be quite clear in our own minds that we are going to set aside a time each day to read about Him so that we may learn to know Him.

Sometimes a couple will come here and tell us that their marriage is going wrong. As we wrote in our first book, *Love that Heals*, often the answer is for them to put aside enough time for each other. The husband may be something of a workaholic, or perhaps the wife may always be tired at the end of the day; consequently they never really have time for each other. Furthermore, the television can be a damaging distraction. It is essential in a marriage for there to be a time, usually in the evening, when the television is turned off, the house is at peace, and the married couple can just enjoy relaxing in each other's company. In the same way, if we are going to take Jesus seriously, when He said that the most important thing in life is for us to love God, we must be sure that we put aside enough time for Him each day. During that time we need to learn to rest in His peace and, indeed, to enjoy being in His company.

But how do we actually love Him? This is a decision. In marriage there are three kinds of love: there is romantic love, when his eyes meet her eyes and time stops still for them. Then there is the friendship which is the love of two people who are companions. But the third love is 'agape' love – the love which takes the decision, the love which says, 'I'm *going* to love the person I'm married to.' Many people have found in marriage counselling that even if the marriage has broken down completely, if the two partners will take the decision with their wills to love each other, first the friendship love comes back and then, in due course, the fullness of the romantic love comes back, too. But it starts with the agape love, the decision of the will that one is going to love the other person.

There is an exact parallel here with our loving the Lord. We need to take the decision to love Him. We may not yet feel any love for Him in our hearts, but that doesn't matter. If we take the decision to love Him, then, in time, the heartfelt love for Him will come.

In marriage it is important for each partner to tell the other of their love for them. As our thanking God for His love becomes part of our regular prayer time, so the awareness of His wonderful love begins to grow in our own hearts. The more we become aware of the wonder of His love for us, the more we find that we are turning to Him and expressing our love for Him ourselves. We need to tell the Lord that we love Him – and the more we tell Him that we love Him, the more our love for Him will in fact grow.

Perhaps we can learn a further lesson from marriage or a close friendship. When we are together with someone we know well and are fond of, it seems natural to chat unselfconsciously with them, and to share what we are thinking with them. We need to get into the way of sharing similarly with the Lord all through the day. Whenever we are alone we can share what we are thinking with Him – we can bring to Him any thought that comes into our minds. We can relate to Him and treat Him as we would a close and intimate friend.

It is not as though we have to manage by ourselves, to love God. We need to keep remembering that there is Someone who is real and who is longing to respond, Himself, and help us to love Him.

As we look round at the world in which we live we see so much suffering. If only people would take Jesus straight – if only they would take Him at His word and seriously set about what He said was the most important thing in life, then how the world would start to change!

CHAPTER 6

# God is More Important than His Work

A lady came to see us who was in distress. She lives alone, has too much time on her hands, and was depressed. 'I keep asking the Lord what He wants me to do with my time,' she said. 'He never seems to answer me, and then whenever I apply even for unpaid work they always turn me down. What can I do?' Clearly she felt that God had given up on her.

We tried to show her that there is one priority in our lives which is even higher than doing God's work, and that is God Himself. In David Watson's last book, *Fear No Evil*, he recounts what was almost a dialogue between himself and God. David was one of the leading evangelists of his day and he prayed to be healed of cancer. He knew that at the age of fifty he could have many more years of active work for the Lord. But he tells how the Lord seemed to be saying to him clearly in prayer that He understood about his ministry, but that His relationship of love with David was even more important. God is indeed more important than His work.

We tried to get this lady to stand aside for a while from her problems (very real though they were). We tried to get her to look at her relationship with God. God hadn't answered her prayer, so far. When she asked Him to guide her in what she should be doing, could it be that God was saying to her, 'I want you to concentrate on Me first, and *then* I will show you what I want you to do'? Certainly it takes a real effort of the will to stand aside from our problems – to let them go – but there is no doubt that if we can do this, and fill our hearts with the presence of the Lord and with His love, we begin to experience His peace again.

This brings wonderful relief, after we have spent so long worrying over our problems and getting nowhere. Moreover, it is as we allow the Lord to fill us with His peace that we begin to hear His still small voice of calm, assurance and certainty. Think of Elijah's experience (1 Kings 19:12).

But we cannot receive His peace if we are rebelling against God. This lady felt that God had given up on her, but in truth she had given up on Him. Because she was no longer 'feeling' His presence, she had stopped trusting Him, and indeed when we asked her, she admitted that her daily prayer time with the Lord was far from what it should be. Many of us rely too much on our feelings, and there are times when I believe the Lord deliberately, and for our own good, withdraws from us the 'feeling' of His presence. We are told that we walk by faith and not by sight (2 Corinthians 5:7). When we don't 'feel' the Lord's loving presence, that is the time for us to proclaim firmly, and preferably aloud, 'I *know* that my Redeemer lives' (Job 19:25) – 'I know that God loves me' (see 1 John 4:19) – 'I know that Jesus promised that if anyone came to Him He would never, never reject them' (see John 6:37, Living Bible). Jesus has made many wonderful promises to us in the Bible and we need to take our stand on them. His promises are so great, compared with our problems. I always love Matthew 11:28, which promises, 'Come to me, all you who are weary and burdened, and I will give you rest.' We do well to keep thanking Him continually for these assurances.

This lady had given up on Him. We had to explain gently that by ceasing to trust Him she had been causing Him pain. If only we could all realise that because He loves us so much, we are able to bring either joy or sadness to the heart of our Lord!

We then reminded her of all her blessings; she seemed to be curiously unaware of them. We live in an age when many of the world's people are hungry, and yet she had never experienced real hunger in her life. When I was a tea planter in the East, after the war, many of the natives lived in huts made of palm fronds, and they were far from waterproof. Many of them slept on the bare earth. When did she give thanks for a sound roof, for a bed to sleep in, and indeed for a change of clothes if she got wet?

We led this lady to repent of her lack of trust in the Lord, to thank Him for all His blessings and to commit herself totally to Him.

We then told her that, when she had exercised faith and taken her stand on the truth of God and of His love, He would restore to her the awareness of His presence – but only in His perfect timing and when in His wisdom He knew she was ready for it.

As she came to turn outwards from herself to the Lord, as she rested in the Lord and as she submitted to Him and ceased to doubt, she would once again hear that gentle but unmistakable inner prompting as He led her lovingly in His way.

In the story of the man who looked back on his life as progress along a sandy beach, Jesus explained why at times there was only a single line of footprints. 'I had not abandoned you at those difficult times in your life,' He said. 'The footprints you see were not yours, but mine. I was carrying you.'

CHAPTER 7

# Help! I've Gone Dry!

Mary (not her real name) is in full-time Christian work and would regard herself as fully committed to the Lord. But she came to us saying that she'd gone dry. Every morning she had to persuade herself when she woke up that God was real, and not just a figment of her imagination. She had no love for Him in her heart. As we talked it began to emerge that the guiding force in her life had become 'I want'. She wanted to feel Jesus' presence in her life, and she wanted to feel loved by Him.

There is nothing wrong with wanting these things, except that wanting them is not the way to get them. Yet how many Christian people live their lives with an ache in their hearts for what they want, and don't seem able to get. How many of them go around like this without ever realising the solution to their problem? We told Mary that she needed to replace the 'I want' in her heart with 'I give'. Giving is the expression of loving. You get love by giving it away. It's no use our deciding to stop wanting. Our minds are not in control of the unconscious depths where the empty ache has its source. But we can decide to redirect our thoughts. We can decide to try and centre our prayers on the words 'I give'. If I take a glass of dirty water and gradually trickle clean water into that glass under the tap, I will eventually have a glass of pure, clean water. As we try and centre our prayers on the words 'I give', in time the ache which says 'I want' will have been replaced.

Jesus says, 'Look, I am standing here, knocking on the door of your heart. I want to come in and enjoy being with you, but are you going to open up your heart to let Me in?' (Revelation 3:20, my paraphrase). Any of us Christians, if asked if we want Jesus to come into our heart, will reply: 'But of course, yes!' We realise readily enough that if Jesus comes into our hearts we will have what we are seeking and the ache of wanting will have been satisfied.

But how do we actually open that door to let Him in? In a sense we can do it just by inviting Him in, in so many words, and yet often there is a further step we need to take.

In a car-park at home the authorities clearly want to be sure that people don't go out through the entrance. There are steel plates let into the surface of the road which, as you go in, will swing down under the wheels of the car as it passes over them, allowing the car to enter. But if you try to go out the same way, you find the steel plates have risen again and your way is blocked; they only swing down one way.

The same is true of the door of our hearts. The way to push down, and hold down, those obstructing plates is by giving ourselves in love to the Lord. As we give, and go on giving, ourselves in love to Him, the plates remain down. Jesus is able to come in with His love, His blessings and His healing and to take up residence in our hearts. But He can't come in unless we, coming from our direction, hold them down. They only swing down in one direction. We hold them down by loving Jesus.

But how do we love Jesus? Let us be sure that we cannot love Him unless we trust Him. And how can we trust Him unless we know what kind of God He is? It is right that in our daily prayers we should thank Him for all that He gives us. But we need to go further than this. We need to thank Him for who He is.

We need continually to be thanking Jesus for the constancy of His love, for His faithfulness towards us, for His perseverance in never letting us go. We need to thank Him for the unbelievable way in which He comes down to our level and is prepared to go grubbing in the muck and the filth of the gutter to find us and rescue us. We need to thank Him for His compassion, for His strength, and for His all-conquering power. We need to thank Him that we can depend on Him completely and rely on Him totally.

We can appreciate Him for who He is, by reading about Him in the Bible, as well as by allowing the Holy Spirit to feed our hearts (although we probably won't realise that He is doing that). But as we thank Him for who He is, we really can't help praising Him, and praising Him from our hearts. We give to Him and we love Him.

As we give ourselves to Him in love, the ache in our hearts melts away and we realise that now He has given us what we have been longing for.

CHAPTER 8

# God Comes to Us in the Stillness

There is nothing wrong with television. But like all of God's gifts it can be misused. At the end of a tiring day we may sink into a comfortable chair, and the easiest thing is just to turn on the television and lose ourselves in what we see on the screen. Sometimes we are actually shutting out God. God only comes to us in the stillness and the quietness. Often it is only when we are alone that we find God.

Here at the London Healing Mission, Audrey and I are pretty tired when we reach the end of the day, but often the Lord will wake me up at about 4 a.m. and it is as if He is saying to me, 'Your need for Me in prayer is greater now than your need for more sleep.' I treasure that hour or so in the middle of the night when the world is hushed and I can be with God. When He has finished with me I can then turn over and sleep soundly till the alarm clock goes.

Elijah had much the same experience. There had been the intense spiritual contest with the powers of darkness on Mount Carmel when

Elijah had challenged the 450 prophets of Baal – and, with God, he won. But so often after a deeply moving spiritual experience there will be a counter-attack from Satan, and by the end of the day Elijah was running for his life (1 Kings 19).

He felt isolated and alone but he was determined to find God. He journeyed for forty days to Mount Horeb, which for generations had been known as the mountain of God.

He took shelter in a cave and a tremendous gale blew through the valley; great trees came crashing down and Elijah cowered in the rear of the cave. But God was not in the gale. Then the mountains began to tremble with a great earthquake. Elijah must have wondered whether the roof of the cave would fall in on him. But God was not in the earthquake. Then, as often happens after an earthquake, there was a forest fire, which raged along the mountainside. But God was not in the fire.

Then Elijah heard the still small voice of God – a gentle whisper – and he knew that in the stillness he had found God. It is in the silence and the quiet that God comes to us.

I find that often I am saying to people, 'Set out deliberately to find the peace of God, "the peace of God which passeth all understanding"' (Philippians 4:7, AV). Not only does God speak to us in the silence and peace but it is then that He nourishes us and builds us up. We find from experience at the Mission that there is much healing in the peace of God. Physically it is in the peace of God that the body's immune system is set free to work at its best, with consequences for our health and our healing.

Often I say to people, 'Study to be like Mary.' Of the two sisters, Martha was always the active one. When their brother Lazarus was seriously ill, it was Martha who went first to meet Jesus while Mary stayed at home (John 11:20). When the two sisters gave a dinner in Jesus' honour the day before His triumphal entry into Jerusalem, Martha was the practical one who was serving while Mary poured the expensive perfume on Jesus' feet and wiped them with her hair (John 12:1–3).

Luke records another occasion when Martha and Mary loaned their home to Jesus (Luke 10:38–42). Martha was getting distracted with all the preparations that needed to be made for supper that evening. Perhaps she had three saucepans on the boil at the same time, the food in the oven was getting overcooked, she had yet to look out a fresh tablecloth, and she would have loved to put some flowers on the table in Jesus' honour but she had not even had time to pick them. Everything that Martha was doing was good. She wanted it to be a really nice evening for Jesus with everything looking its best.

But Mary was apparently idling away the time just sitting with Jesus. Surely Mary shared Martha's desire to have a really nice supper for Him? Surely it was right for Mary to stop sitting around, and share with her, Martha, the work of getting everything ready? Martha has so much of our sympathy as she rushes round doing all the good and necessary things to prepare the evening meal. But 'Mary has chosen what is better,' Jesus said.

So much of what we do in our homes and

churches is good and needful. But when Mary sat at Jesus' feet listening to Him, Jesus said that that was the better choice and He would not stop her.

How much more effective we would be in our daily lives if we had the courage to stop being busy with non-essentials and instead sought the quietness and peace where we, too, might be like Mary and sit listening to Jesus.

CHAPTER 9

# Difficulty with 'Love'

So often, people who have been emotionally damaged have difficulty with the word 'love'. George (not his real name) was one of them. I knew that George had had a traumatic childhood. His first marriage had been a failure and he was now struggling with his second marriage. I had started talking to him about the love of Jesus when he interrupted me.

'What actually is love?' he asked.

I thought, and then replied: 'Love is when you give yourself to someone and when you try and help them.' Then I realised what lay behind his question. George was really asking me, 'What do you actually mean when you say that *Jesus* loves *me*?'

'It means that He cares very deeply for you,' I continued. 'It means that He treasures you, that you are of value to Him, and that He just wants to pour Himself out, in comforting you, helping you and strengthening you.'

George thought for a bit. Then I realised that he was saying something under his breath. It was the same thing, repeated over and over again. I listened carefully and I was able to pick up the words,

'I'm not worthy, I'm not worthy, I'm not worthy....'

'Of course you're not worthy,' I said. 'Nor am I. The only reason that Jesus could love people like you and me is because He's divine, and He loves with a love which is divine.'

Another silence followed. Then, once again, I realised George was saying something to himself. Again, as I listened, I picked up the words: 'I can't, I can't, I can't....'

'Do you realise,' I asked George, 'that you, who have been rejected so much in your life, are now actually rejecting Jesus, when you say that you can't accept His love for you? Do you realise,' I asked, 'that in rejecting Jesus you are actually inflicting on Him the same hurt that others have inflicted so often on you?'

George is a man who stands well over six feet tall but, at these words, he crumpled up and sobbed. I think probably for the first time ever he was really open to receiving the love of Jesus.

He realised, however, that before long he would have to face up to going back home. His wife, too, had been deeply rejected and hurt, and I think probably it was one of those marriages where each of the partners was rejecting the other, and thus hurting the other.

'What do I do', George asked me, 'when she rejects my love and it is really like a knife going right through me?' It is so easy for us to answer glibly that a person should let go of the hurt to Jesus. But how does one explain in practical terms how to do this? I put it to George like this:

**(1)** Remember that Jesus loves you with a love which is, quite simply, perfect. Remember that because He is God He loves you 'on the inside'. He

can see right into your heart and He is aware of all the hurt that is there.
**(2)** When we see somebody we love being cruelly treated, we may find ourselves saying that our hearts are 'bleeding' for that person. In exactly the same way when Jesus is aware – as He is – of the pain and turmoil in our hearts, His very heart is bleeding for us. Indeed, He is suffering the same hurt in His own heart as we are suffering in ours, precisely because of His great tenderness and love for us.
**(3)** If we can pray through this fact, we can come to the point where, although we are still conscious of our hurt, we become aware that we are not alone with it. As we reflect that His own heart is bleeding for us, we realise that He is with us in our hurt, because He is feeling it, too.
**(4)** As we dwell on this fact, as we continue to thank Him for His love and for His compassion for us, as we thank Him that He is, indeed, suffering the same hurt in His heart because of His love for us, we can then begin to let the hurt go to Him within that shared experience of pain.

It is wrong to bottle up emotions. The way to get rid of hurt is to let it go to Jesus.

Then we need to get on with the on-going prayer: 'Thank You so much, Jesus, for the wonderful way in which You actually love me.' Thus we receive His love for us, in faith. If we can really receive His love and can let go of our own hurt, we're well on the way to loving our neighbour, without fear of our neighbour rejecting us.

George left me that day more at peace, and indeed happier, deep within himself, than I'd ever known him before.

CHAPTER 10

# Faith

'You of little faith,' said Jesus to His disciples. But faith is not easy. I have always had a certain sympathy for the cynical young man who said, 'Faith is being able to make yourself believe what you know is not true.'

Jesus never said we needed to have great faith in God. I remember when Jim Glennon told us about a present a friend had given him. When he opened the present it appeared to be a perfectly ordinary jam jar, clean and empty. Jim was at a loss to know what to say. After all, it isn't easy to enthuse about an empty jam jar. 'But how wonderfully clean it is!' is about all one can say; or else, 'You have polished it beautifully.'

But as he hesitated, his friend told him that he hadn't in fact given him an empty jam jar. Jim was mystified. As far as he was aware the only thing the jam jar contained was air.

'But look right in the bottom of the jar,' his friend said. As Jim looked carefully he thought he detected a tiny spot of dust, and he remarked on this to his friend. 'That isn't a speck of dust,' his friend said. 'That is a mustard seed.'

Jesus told us that we did not need to have great

faith, just faith as big – or as small – as a mustard seed. We don't need great faith in God. What we need is faith in a great God.

Many people are helped by the story of the desperate father who asked Jesus (after the Transfiguration) if He could heal his son and set him free.

'"Everything is possible for him who believes," said Jesus. Immediately the boy's father exclaimed, "I do believe; help me overcome my unbelief!"' (Mark 9:23–24).

I believe, if we translate the father's remark into everyday language, he was saying something like this: 'Jesus, I want to believe, but I have got this rotten great lump of unbelief in me and you will have to help me cope with that.'

For me the point of the story is that that attitude of mind in the father was sufficient for Jesus to heal his son. Many people have been helped when they have come to realise that, if they can say what that father said 2000 years ago, they have got enough faith.

There is a sense in which faith is indeed the ability to make oneself believe what one 'knows' is not true; it all depends what one means by 'oneself'. There is alive in me – all too alive! – the old fallen self who looks at everything from an earthly point of view and says, 'I won't believe what I can't see.'

At the same time there is the new creation in each of us, a new creation which comes from God and believes the things of the Spirit. In many ways faith involves a decision not to listen to the old self but to believe what is set out in the Bible and what is spoken by the Holy Spirit. It all depends which voice one listens to.

I used to regard faith as one of those difficult 'religious' words. But I was helped by reading Alan Dale's Bible for children. He leaves out the word 'faith' altogether, and instead uses the word 'trust'. If we can come to know that God is always and invariably a God of perfect love and that He longs to do what is good and perfect for His children, then we can trust Him. If we can trust Him we are indeed then having faith.

A woman came here recently who apparently made a habit of badgering God. Her husband was an unbeliever and so she walked out into the open air one day and really wrestled with God. 'Now look here, God,' she said, 'You have given me passages in Scripture about casting mountains into the sea; now I want you to get a move on and open my husband's heart so that he may accept You as his Lord!' Within a few weeks he did. Often we are not bold enough in our praying. We need to remember that there is no documentary evidence of Jesus telling His disciples to pray for the sick. His words were simple: 'Go and heal them!' St Matthew quotes Jesus as saying the time has come when 'forceful men lay hold of' the kingdom of heaven (Matthew 11:12).

Let us accept that we have enough faith, and let us get on and use it!

CHAPTER 11

# Praying in the Name of Jesus

A couple of years ago I was talking to a clergyman who is himself in the healing ministry. We got round to the question of praying in power. 'I didn't know,' he said, 'that there is power in the name of Jesus.' Is this just a theological nicety such as clergymen like to mull over when two of them get together? Or is it a matter of vital importance to the church today?

I'm afraid we have to accept that some of the churches in this country, and indeed overseas, are not very effective. Well do I remember Reg East, who used to head the community at Whatcombe House, saying of his first parish: 'We put a new roof on the church and we put in a new organ, but then I realised that what we were missing was renewed people.'

What is needed, if the church is to be regarded as other than a harmless irrelevance, is for the power to come back into the body of Christ. Jesus said to His followers: 'You will receive power when the Holy Spirit comes on you' (Acts 1:8). Paul wrote to the church in Corinth, 'The kingdom of God is not a matter of talk but of power' (1 Corinthians 4:20). The Bible tells us that in the last days men will have a form of godliness but denying its power (2 Timothy 3:5). We have only to read through the book of Acts to be reminded that the early church well knew the power of Jesus. The church desperately needs that same power today.

The scriptural bases for saying that the power is in the name of Jesus are many. Minutes before Jesus ascended into heaven He said to His disciples, 'All authority in heaven and on earth has been given to me' (Matthew 28:18; other translations use the words 'all power').

At the end of Mark's Gospel, Jesus says that 'these signs will accompany those who believe', and He mentions, among others, driving out demons, speaking in new tongues and placing their hands on sick people that they may get well. But the sentence begins with the words spoken by Jesus, 'In my name they will ...' (Mark 16:17–18).

Perhaps the best-known verse in the New Testament is John 3:16 – 'God so loved the world that he gave his one and only Son, that whoever believes in him shall not perish but have eternal life.' It was a long time before I realised that belief in God is not actually the fundamental which gives us eternal life. It is belief in Jesus. John goes on: 'For God did not send his Son into the world to condemn the world, but to save the world through him. Whoever believes in him is not condemned, but whoever does not believe stands condemned already because he has not believed in the name of God's one and only Son' (John 3:17–18).

In the same way we read in Romans 10:9, 'If you confess with your mouth, "Jesus is Lord," and believe in your heart that God raised him from the dead, you will be saved.'

But if it be true that the power is in the name of Jesus, what about those who rejoice in praying to their heavenly Father? It must be right for us to pray to our heavenly Father, for Jesus said to the disciples, 'This is how you should pray: "Our Father in heaven ..."' (Matthew 6:9). We need to keep this truth in balance with the fact of the power being in the name of Jesus.

The early church in Jerusalem knew this well. At the beginning of the book of Acts, Luke tells us that in his first book he wrote about 'all that Jesus began to do and to teach until the day when he was taken up to heaven'. We know from the internal evidence that Luke researched his material carefully before writing his two books. From this verse we see the conclusion he came to, namely, that the whole of Jesus' earthly ministry was only as it were the first act in the drama. He knew that the power of Jesus continued after His death and resurrection, through His followers, the early church.

As we read on in the book of Acts, we read about Pentecost and Peter's sermon. We read that the people were cut to the heart and said to Peter: '"Brothers, what shall we do?" Peter replied, "Repent and be baptised, every one of you, in the name of Jesus Christ"' (Acts 2:37–38).

Only a few verses later there is the account of how the cripple at the Gate Beautiful of the Temple sought alms from Peter and John. Peter's reply still rings down the centuries: 'Silver or gold I do not have, but what I have I give you. In the name of Jesus Christ of Nazareth, walk.' A few minutes later, when he was explaining to the crowd what had happened, he said: 'By faith in the name of Jesus, this man whom you see and know was made strong. It is Jesus' name and the faith that comes through him that has given this complete healing to him, as you can all see' (Acts 3:16).

Not long afterwards, when the apostles had been miraculously released from jail, and were had up by the authorities, Peter was quite clear in what he said: 'God exalted [Jesus] to his own right hand as Prince and Saviour that he might give repentance and forgiveness of sins to Israel' (Acts 5:31).

Some while later, Saul (as he was then) had his tremendous experience on the road to Damascus, and he was blinded. When Ananias came to him, his words were, 'The Lord – Jesus, who appeared to you on the road as you were coming here – has sent me so that you may see again' (Acts 9:17).

Again, when Paul and Silas had been miraculously released from prison, the jailer, who was terrified, cried out, 'What must I do to be saved?' They replied, 'Believe in the Lord Jesus, and you will be saved' (Acts 16:31).

I give you three more brief quotations: 'Thanks be to God! He gives us the victory through our Lord Jesus Christ' (1 Corinthians 15:57). 'God exalted [Jesus] to the highest place and gave him the name that is above every name, that at the name of Jesus every knee should bow, in heaven and on earth and under the earth, and every tongue confess that Jesus

Christ is Lord' (Philippians 2:9–11). Finally, the closing words of the Bible: 'He who testifies to these things says: "Yes, I am coming soon." Amen. Come, Lord Jesus. The grace of the Lord Jesus be with God's people. Amen' (Revelation 22:20–21).

Yet I find it useful to 'earth' what we read in the Bible in our daily experience. We need to acknowledge the Lordship of Jesus if we are to minister and preach with power. God grant that more and more churches throughout the land will learn to use the power in the name of Jesus, and will thus come to stand out as beacons of God's light in the darkness which surrounds them.

CHAPTER 12

# What I Have, I Give

In the early years of the Christian church they used to tell a legend of when Jesus was a small boy. With a group of His little friends He was apparently playing on the bank of the local river. The ground there was of clay and, as country children will do, they were mixing some of the clay with the river water and making little models.

'Let's each make a model of a bird!' one of the boys cried out. After a while one of the boys, younger than the rest, started to cry. His companions' models were beginning to look something like birds, but, try as he would, the model he was making still looked like a misshapen lump of clay. The tears began to roll down his cheeks.

In his distress he picked up the lump of clay and went over to Jesus. He handed the lump of clay to Him. 'You try and make something of it,' he said.

Jesus felt sorry for him. He reached out His hand, so the story goes, and touched the lump of clay. It shook itself; it spread its wings, and then a beautiful bird flew up into the air, circled round the little boy's head and then settled on his shoulder.

I doubt if the story is true. It sounds too much like magic. But I do think the story teaches us a valuable lesson. If we will bring what we have got to Jesus, however little it is, He will touch it, and transform it.

Let us move forward some 1200 or 1300 years, to France, where the French king ruled in all his majesty and pomp. Sometimes in a medieval court the ceremonial became heavy and it was then that the court jester, or the court 'fool' as he was sometimes known, came into his own. At a particularly solemn moment he would turn a couple of cartwheels on the floor of the great hall. Or, if one of the great nobles was becoming too serious, he might look up and see the court fool standing on his head in front of him.

The story concerns a prior of Notre Dame at Cluny – and I believe this story is true. One day he went into the church, magnificent with all its gold paint, its brilliantly coloured enamels, and the beautiful embroideries on the seats and the kneelers. Then he looked up and, to his horror, he saw the fool turning cartwheels in front of the high altar. As he watched, the fool stopped and solemnly stood on his head.

The prior strode angrily up the aisle and seized the man by the shoulder. 'Whatever are you doing with your antics, profaning this holy place?' he shouted.

The poor fool looked very crestfallen. At last he stammered: 'I had nothing else to give Him. I thought perhaps I could do my tricks for Him and He would accept that from me.'

The great prior has been forgotten for centuries, but the story of the Jongleur de Dieu has blessed countless people down the years. If we give whatever we have got – however little – to Jesus, He will reach out His hand, bless it and use it to His glory.

One of my favourite people in the Bible is a boy whose name we do not even know. It was on the occasion when Jesus saw a great crowd coming towards Him on a lonely hillside and He had turned to Philip saying, 'How are we to feed them?' (John 6). Philip was nonplussed. Andrew then told Jesus that he had found one boy who was willing to give up his picnic – just five small rolls and a couple of the local fish.

The little boy can have had no idea of the miracle which the young Teacher was going to perform, and in giving all that he had to Jesus he faced the prospect of going home with an empty tummy. But he gave Jesus what he had. We know the rest of the story. Jesus reached out His hands and gave thanks for the five loaves and the two small fishes. After Jesus had prayed, the little boy's offering was sufficient to feed all that great crowd of people.

We see the same message throughout the Bible, when people who had so little to offer just surrendered themselves to God. When God called Gideon to lead the Israelites to freedom from the host of Midian, Gideon protested: 'My clan is the weakest in Manasseh, and I am the least in my family' (Judges 6:15). Yet, however little he seemed to have, he surrendered himself to God, and God used him.David was the same. When the Israelites were standing in terror before Goliath and the Philistine army, David's father had called down eight of his sons to military service, but he hadn't even bothered to call the shepherd boy. Yet David, small as he was, made himself available to God – and how He used him! In the same way, when Peter and John were had up before the religious authorities for healing the cripple at the Gate Beautiful of the Temple, the authorities saw that they were just ordinary, uneducated men. But they had made themselves available to the Lord and, as they surrendered themselves to Him, how powerfully He was able to use them.

I like the story of the little peasant girl, Albanian by race, who was born some eighty years ago in a remote village in the mountains. What chance had a peasant girl from the back of beyond of doing anything much for Jesus? Yet she gave Him all she had, which was herself, and most of us will know her as Mother Teresa of Calcutta.

Where does this touch you and me? If we will surrender ourselves to Jesus, He will accept us and He will use us to His glory. But so often a waiting period is involved while He prepares us.

For the last seven years of my first career, which was in a financial group in the City of London, I knew that sooner or later the Lord was going to call me out to work for Him. But it took seven years of preparing before I was ready to be used by Him. I had a letter the other day from a woman in East Anglia, who has had to give up her career as a professional piano teacher and is just waiting to be used in healing by Jesus. She wrote to me saying: 'I have given myself to Him. What do I do now?'

So often the answer is for us to be patient, to be

submissive to Him and just get on with growing in the knowledge and love of Jesus, as one day follows another. Often it is a help to live as if each day is going to be our last one on earth. That helps us to surrender everything to Him in love and worship.

If we do this patiently, then, in His own perfect timing, He will lead us into His work. He will multiply out of all recognition the little which we have been able to give Him. Whether He touches the little lump of clay, the fool's antics, the little boy's picnic, or ourselves, He transforms what we have given to Him and uses it more wonderfully than we could ever imagine.

Meanwhile, we need to pray continually, 'Lord, I just want to love You, to follow You and to serve You.'

CHAPTER 13

# 'Unless You Become Like Little Children'

Jesus said: 'Unless you change and become like little children, you will never enter the kingdom of heaven' (Matthew 18:3). There are moments when one is inclined to feel that some of Jesus' sayings were rather far-fetched. After all, we live in an age when we are encouraged to stand on our own feet, to be assertive and to make a success of things, and here is Jesus apparently saying that we've got to go back to being children. My own recollection of childhood is of being told by grown-ups that this was the best part of one's life, whilst my reaction was always to retort, 'I can't wait to be grown-up!'

Yet, once again, one is brought up short by the question, 'What do you make of Jesus?' Was Jesus a young man who knew what He was talking about? Yes.

Here Jesus lays down the condition for my going to heaven. What if I don't go to heaven? Think of spending all eternity estranged from God. The thought is too ghastly even to consider. So what is this condition Jesus is saying I must fulfil if I am to enter the kingdom of heaven?

When Jesus said that we must become like little children again, I believe He had in mind the way children accept things without questioning. Yet we live in an age when so many children have been damaged emotionally by rejection or by being abandoned, by one parent or both. Because of the emotional hurt, children often lose their childlike qualities at an early age. Indeed, there are many cases where the emotional damage to the child starts with its mother's rejection before it is born. But the child, while still childlike, has a capacity for accepting things without questioning which is usually lost in the grown-up, and here is Jesus saying that we must seek to regain that childlike quality.

I think of Tom, aged twelve, who came to one of our Healing Services. His mother had brought him because she was worried about a hacking cough which he had had night and day for months, and for which the specialists had found no cure. Tom came up to the altar rail to Audrey, my wife, for prayer.

'What do you want prayer for?' Audrey asked him. He explained about the cough. Audrey asked him what Jesus was going to do. 'Why, heal it of course!' Tom retorted. She prayed for him quite briefly and then Tom went back to rejoin his mother at the back of the chapel.

'What happened when she prayed for you?' his mother asked. 'Well, of course Jesus healed me!' Tom replied. He never coughed again.

Often when one is praying for children one can turn it into a game. Audrey and I remember a lovely little red-haired girl of seven whom we were asked to pray for, as she was suffering from recurrent nightmares. The three of us had fun together as we asked Jesus to station a big angel with a drawn sword at each of the four corners of her bed to keep anything harmful away from her, and then together we asked Jesus that she might rest in peace through the night.

We learned later that the nightmares stopped from the evening we prayed. That girl had the ability to accept what we were praying for, without questioning.

But when Jesus told us that we must become like little children, I believe there was another quality which we find in the very small child and which He must have had in mind. The small child, before it learns to the contrary from experience, instinctively feels that its parents must be perfect. The small child trusts its parents completely. They are there to look after it and to provide everything that it needs and, indeed, to have the answer to all its questions.

So many grown-ups are worried and anxious, and the answer to their problems is for them to ask Jesus for a simple childlike trust to grow in them – but a trust not in their parents but in Him who is truly perfect.

The quality in small children which Jesus specifically mentioned was that of humility. The small child doesn't put on airs. The small child trusts its parents and respects them. We find in ministry here that it is absolutely essential for us to humble ourselves completely before the Lord. If ever any vestige of pride lodges in us we know that the power goes right out of our ministry.

We do, indeed, live in an age when children are

being damaged often at an early age through abuse, whether verbal or physical, or through rejection. At the same time, there is evidence that the Lord is using children with a greater degree of power than we have seen hitherto. One of our team was worshipping in a fellowship at Kansas City. He saw an enormous American man, perhaps weighing twenty stone, lying slumped over a chair, 'out' under the power of the Holy Spirit. He had been prayed down in the Holy Spirit by two seven-year-old girls.

I think of a girl who is now eight who joined with some of her friends at a recent New Wine Christian Festival to pray for one of their number who couldn't see properly. After the children had prayed with her, she could see.

I think then of another child aged seven at the time, who, during break in the school playground, met one of her class who was suffering from nightmares. She asked Jesus to release her from the nightmares, and the nightmares stopped.

We can't change ourselves and make ourselves once more like little children, but Jesus can. Moreover, if we pray for what is humanly impossible, and if we know that we are praying in line with His will, then we know that Jesus in His perfect way will answer our prayer. Unless we become like little children, He said, we won't enter the kingdom of heaven.

CHAPTER 14

# On Accepting Jesus' Love

Although we counsel people, we see the counselling as being only one prong of a two-pronged ministry – and in fact, the lesser of the two prongs. We often say the real power comes during the subsequent time of prayer. Indeed, because of this, we always think of ourselves as 'ministering' to people, rather than just 'counselling'. Incidentally, we have yet to think of a suitable word to cover those we are ministering to. 'Ministerees' is just possible, though it is an ugly word!

When a person makes an appointment with one or two of the team at the Mission, he, or she, has a one-and-a-half-hour session, and everything is of course completely confidential. Whilst the person is talking, we are always trying to discern the root cause of the problem. Quite often it is not anything which they have mentioned at all. Yet, when we bring it out, their eyes light up and they say, 'Yes, yes, that's it!'

Sometimes we will pick up from a chance remark that, underneath, the person is suffering, say, from a sense of guilt. But even this may not really be the root of the problem. Often a person believes that they can't be forgiven because they cannot accept that they can be loved. This can lead to them having a poor image of themselves, with destructive consequences.

How can we help people to realise they are loved by the One Who is perfect love? How can one help them to believe that the Lord accepts them as they are and loves them with a love which is unconditional? How can one help them to see that literally neither death nor life nor anything else in all creation will be able to separate them from the love of God (Romans 8:37–39)?

There are several ways we can tackle this problem. Often one can challenge a person with the question: 'Don't you believe your Bible?' If the person says he does, one can lead him through the various passages which assure him of God's love, and help him to take them in.

But he may well reply: 'I know this in my head, but it's in my heart that I am hurting. How do I believe it in my heart?' It is a psychological fact that a truth which is often repeated becomes accepted. We may say to the person: 'Basing yourself on what you know in your head to be true, will you acknowledge every ten minutes or so of your waking day that Jesus loves you?' It may only take one second to pause momentarily and say, either aloud or under one's breath: 'Thank You, Jesus, that You love me.' It's no use waiting until one 'feels' like saying it! It is an act of the will. Thanking Jesus for His love every ten minutes adds up to about a hundred times a day. We call it the 'Hundred Times' prayer.

Once we can help someone to accept that Jesus

loves him as he is, his whole attitude to life gradually changes. When someone has taken in this fundamental truth, he can't have a poor self-image! 'If you're good enough to be loved by Jesus Himself, how *can* you complain about yourself?' we ask. Sometimes, to make the point, we ask: 'Do you think the Lord made a mistake when He made you as you are, instead of making you in the same mould as these other people you seem to envy so much?' Or again, 'Can't you accept that God knows His job better than you do?' It is a short step to a variation of the 'Hundred Times' prayer, namely: 'Thank You, Jesus, that You chose to make me as I am.'

If a failure to accept His love leads to a poor self-image, it can often lead, too, to a crippling sense of guilt. Nowadays we are told that we must help people to forgive themselves. One can try and persuade oneself that one forgives oneself, but usually this simply means that one is condoning the failure or the sin. Condoning it is not washing it away. We forget what the Jews saw clearly 2000 years ago – that only God can forgive sins. God will not forgive our sins unless we face up to them as being sins, unless we repent of them as sins, and unless we ask Him to forgive us. Then He does forgive us.

I doubt if our repentance achieves very much unless we accept His forgiveness. Our authority for doing this is contained in many biblical passages, one of these being 1 John 1:9: 'If we confess our sins, he is faithful and just and will forgive us our sins and purify us from all unrighteousness.' Getting someone to repent is not a degrading business of rubbing their nose in the mud.

Repentance is the key which enables people to receive the freedom and joy which Jesus longs to give, as He releases His forgiveness upon them.

Perhaps, however, His forgiveness is only accepted as head knowledge. Then, once again, we say the 'Hundred Times' prayer: 'Thank You, Jesus, that You have forgiven me and set me free from guilt.'

A professional psychiatrist said to me: 'If we could only get across to the patients in psychiatric hospitals that Jesus forgives them, half the beds would be emptied overnight!' There is healing in the Lord's forgiveness. We see this clearly in the story of the paralytic who was lowered by his friends through a hole in the roof so that they could get him to Jesus.

But the root cause of a person's problems often lies in his inability to accept that he is loved by Jesus. Once he can accept the love of Jesus he begins to respond, and to love Him. Truth is eternal, and John expressed this when he wrote: 'We love because he first loved us' (1 John 4:19).

The basis of our approach in ministry is to help a person to get right in his love relationship with the Lord. I remember saying to Virginia, one of the Healing Mission team, 'Surely you've been married long enough to know that Jesus has to come first in your life, and your husband, Michael, second?' After a moment's thought she replied, 'But, Andy, of course I know that if I become unplugged from Jesus, I'm no use to Michael!' In our counselling and, indeed, in our praying too, we are always seeking to help the person to 'plug in' more closely to Jesus and draw more on the healing power of His love.

However, I think of Fred (not his real name), a seventy-year-old bachelor. He had had some Sunday school training but I don't think he had given another thought to the Christian faith for sixty years. I talked to him about the love of Jesus, but realised that, in his case, I was getting nowhere.

I prayed therefore for his leg, which was hurting; indeed, he had only been able to walk in with the aid of a walking frame. After prayer we went on chatting and I noticed him rubbing his leg, rather absent-mindedly. I asked what he was doing.

'It's funny,' he said, 'but there's a kind of warmth running up and down my leg.'

I guessed what the Lord was doing! 'Try standing up,' I suggested.

He got to his feet, saying, 'Well, that's odd – I couldn't do that before.'

I held on to his walking frame and told him to walk up and down the room. As he did so, the excitement in him mounted.

'Can I go upstairs now?' he asked.

'Of course!'

He ran up the first flight and called over the banisters, 'Can I go up the next flight?'

'Of course!' I said again.

As the Lord healed his leg, some deep spiritual healing took place. When Fred left the Mission he was praising Jesus.

We don't worry whether or not those who come to us are Christians. What does worry us is if they leave the Healing Mission as non-Christians!

Betty (not her real name) was one of the many who felt it was beyond her to accept that she was loved by Jesus. Aged forty, she had been a depress-ive for many years. Her self-image was low and there was a sense of guilt. We talked about the love of Jesus for her and she said she would try the 'Hundred Times' prayer, but she was far from being convinced. We stood up to pray.

When we pray with people we may remind them of sunbathing on a hot summer's day. They relax and let the warmth of the sun soak into them. In some ways that is a description of what prayer should be like. We relax and allow the warmth of Jesus' love to soak into us. Again, there is a parallel with a flower in the garden. Some flowers turn towards the sun and open their petals. They receive the living light of the sun.

So in praying with people we deliberately try to help them to open their hearts to Jesus – to let go of any restraint or sin, or painful memories, and to let his healing love soak in. We prayed this way with Betty. As sometimes happens, she fell to the floor under the power of the Holy Spirit. She lay there, her face transformed with the most beauti-ful smile, and we heard her quietly say, 'Oh Jesus, how I love You!' Through the power of the Holy Spirit she had been enabled to accept His love and now *she* loved *Him*.

CHAPTER 15

# Power in Prayer

A vicar calling on some of his parishioners went to see a lady in her nineties. The vicar must have been forty or fifty years younger than she was, and the lady was a little put out when he started asking her about her prayer life.

'But of course I say my prayers every day,' she assured the vicar, believing that would put an end to the conversation. But the vicar pressed on: 'When you say your prayers, what actually do you say?'

'I always say what I was taught to say,' the old lady replied. 'I always start my prayers by saying, "God bless Mummy and Daddy".' Like the rest of us, she needed to keep her prayer life under review.

If our prayers are proving ineffective we may need to do something about it. Supposing a lady has an electric mixer in her kitchen and it breaks down. She doesn't just wring her hands and say, 'Oh dear, it doesn't work.' If she has a husband who is skilled in these matters she will ask him to put her mixer right. If she is like Audrey in having a husband who is unskilled, she will send for the electrician. What she will not do is sit there, wringing her hands and bewailing the fact that the mixer does not work.

Yet that is the attitude so many Christians adopt where their prayer life is concerned. If your prayer life isn't working there are only two possible reasons. Either God has got it wrong, or you have. Of those two alternatives one is a good deal more probable than the other.

A lady came to see me recently, her mind full of her problems. She started telling me her life story, beginning in April 1959. When she had covered April, she moved on to May 1959, and she then started on June. At that point I had to remind her that I couldn't give her the whole day. She went on to assure me how religious she was, that she went to Mass every morning of her life, and she told me at length about how she prayed for each of her children, for each of her grandchildren, for her church, for the country and many other worthy causes.

I said to her, 'Your trouble is that you are "praying" too much.' I meant that she was going through an interminable shopping list with God, and was still left with the burden of her hurts over the last thirty-odd years. Because her mind rotated endlessly on her problems and on her efforts to 'pray', she was strung up and on edge.

I told her that she needed to seek the peace of God and to learn to rest in His presence. Nobody had ever told her that real prayer is enjoying being with Jesus. We stopped the recital of her life story and we prayed for half an hour, helping her to let go of her problems and to drink in the peace and the healing of Jesus. Her sister told me two days later how greatly it had helped her, as she released the hurts to Jesus, and allowed Him to come to her with His peace and His inner healing.

For many of us prayer is an exercise of the will, a trudge through certain predetermined steps. Often we don't give God time to respond to us. Much of prayer should be waiting on Him and allowing Him to come to us. Often we need to seek His stillness and to allow Him to take the initiative Himself, as He releases His peace upon us.

Yet at other times we do need to wrestle with God in prayer. We read in Genesis 32 how Jacob wrestled through the night in prayer, refusing to let God go until He had blessed him. In the same way Jesus told His followers that 'forceful men' are laying hold of the kingdom of heaven (Matthew 11:12). There are times in prayer when we need to bang on the gates of heaven, crying out, 'Lord, I want!' – and indeed sometimes going further and saying, 'Lord, I claim...'.

A woman came to see Audrey a short while ago. Her marriage was on the rocks and the previous week her husband had told her over breakfast that he was seeing a solicitor that morning to file for divorce. He had had enough of her, he said, and he had decided to free himself from their marriage.

The woman told Audrey how she went out into the fields that morning, and for an hour or more, literally shouted at God, reminding Him that He hated divorce, that He had brought her husband and her together in the first place, and demanding the healing of their marriage!

That afternoon when her husband returned he seemed thoughtful. Within a few minutes he turned to his wife, saying to her, 'I have changed my mind. I don't want to leave you and I have told the lawyers that I wish to drop the divorce proceedings.' There are times when it is right for us to bang on the gates of heaven.

But there is another side to this matter. Often we think of being passive and being positive as opposites, but I believe the Christian needs to be both. It is no good shouting at God unless we know that what we are demanding is in line with His will. John tells us in his first letter, 'If we ask anything according to his will, he hears us. And if we know that he hears us ... we know that we have what we asked of him' (1 John 5:14–15). We need first to be passive before God, listening to Him in the stillness, so that we may learn what His will is in the situation. Then indeed we can step out and be positive, demanding that God bring about what we have felt is His desire.

Yet even when we are hearing God's will correctly we need to be careful that we are not bringing our own will into play. It is no good our trying to push God around. God is sovereign and we must always be submissive to His will. A husband and wife came to one of our services, she having three weeks to live because of terminal cancer. Audrey actually never prayed for her but she helped the man to release his wife to Jesus. He had been willing her healing, and it was that which was actually blocking Jesus' healing power. Three weeks later they returned to give thanks for she had been miraculously healed. We need to discern His will and then perhaps to demand that His will be done, while never seeking to pressurise Him, for then our will can block His healing power.

Often we are praying in the quietness of our own room. But there are times when we pray for people in their presence. At these times we need to remember that there is never any need to shout. The power of prayer is not enhanced by the amount of noise we make. What is necessary is to speak the word of God. That may be a quotation from the Bible, or words that the Holy Spirit has given us a moment before. We need to speak His word, strong in the assurance of God's own promise. Isaiah quotes God as saying, 'My word ... will not return to me empty, but will accomplish what I desire and achieve the purpose for which I sent it' (Isaiah 55:11).

If our praying is proving ineffective we will be the ones who have got it wrong, and we may need to review our approach to prayer.

CHAPTER 16

# Why Does God Allow Suffering?

'With all the suffering there is in the world today, how can you honestly tell me that there is a God of love behind it all? If there is such a God, why does He ever allow it?' Many a good, decent person today will reject the claims of Christianity because he cannot find a satisfactory answer to these questions.

But the matter goes deeper. I don't believe that we who are Christians can really pray effectively unless we have ourselves faced up to the question: How do we reconcile all the suffering in the world with the existence of a God of perfect love? If there is in our minds any doubt as to whether He really is a God of perfect love, in whom we can put all our trust, we shall never be able to pray to Him with confidence. We read in Hebrews 11 that without faith it is impossible to please God. That means trusting Him. Unless we are completely sure of His abiding goodness, we cannot fully trust Him when we pray to Him, and then our prayers will lack effectiveness.

I don't believe there is a complete answer to the

question. After all, the greater part of the book of Job is occupied with the question, 'Why do I suffer?', and God never gives Job the answer. Yet I believe we can shed some light on the problem.

Let us take first the suffering which comes when we deliberately disobey God. If I were to go out and get blind drunk, I would suffer from a hangover the following morning. I don't think any of us would see any injustice in that suffering. In it we would see the guiding hand of God. In a similar way, if a young man on the threshold of adult life resolves that whatever is going to happen in life he is going to be happy, we all know that he will finish up being a selfish misery. His suffering will come on him as a direct result of his having turned his back on God and sought his own ends.

It is harder to explain suffering when a person is the innocent victim of someone else's misdeeds. I think few of us would deny that there have been times in our lives when we have hurt others. Yet if I were to be so programmed that I was not able to hurt anyone else, I would cease to be a real person. I would just be a puppet, dancing as some superior power pulled the strings. Moreover, if I were programmed so that I had no freedom of choice between good and bad, I would be unable to love, for love has to be given freely. In brief, if I were programmed so that I was incapable of hurting other people, I do not believe I would really be able to help them either. I can only say that I am utterly thankful to the Lord for letting me be a real person, with freedom of choice between wrong and right – despite the fact that I may misuse that freedom. I believe most of the suffering in the world stems, directly or indirectly, from the misuse of our free will. And, for better or worse, God will always respect our free will.

Let us then consider a third category of suffering: the suffering which comes from natural disasters. How can a God of love allow that suffering?

I think we have a clue when Paul writes to the Romans of the hope 'that the creation itself will be liberated from its bondage to decay and brought into the glorious freedom of the children of God. We know that the whole creation has been groaning, as in the pains of childbirth, right up to the present time' (Romans 8:21–22).

We realise that somehow at the time of the fall, humankind rejected the divine inheritance and turned their backs on God. As a result, all of us face suffering. But I believe it went further than that. I believe that somehow the fall encompassed the whole of creation. I believe that is the underlying reason for the injustice of natural disasters.

We seem to get confirmation of this view when we read in the Old Testament that if God's people will return to Him and accept Him as their God, they will prosper and their crops will not fail nor their cattle miscarry. There seems to be a connection between our turning to God and protection from at any rate some natural disasters (e.g., Deuteronomy 28:3–5).

But I don't believe that any consideration of the place of suffering in our lives is complete unless we ask ourselves, 'How is God Himself affected by our suffering?' If He is a God of love, He must be feeling for each of His people in their suffering. His very heart must be bleeding for them in their pain. We often forget that God Himself shares in the suffering of His people precisely because He loves them so much.

Towards the end of the book of Job, Job has come to the end of his questioning. At last, and for the first time, he falls silent and it is only then that he begins to be able to hear God. He becomes aware of the wonder and the majesty of God, and in the presence of God he repents of all his questioning.

Then three things happen. First (by inference) his suffering ceases. Secondly, he makes the tremendous transition from being someone who has 'heard about' God to being someone who now can say, 'I know God' (literally: 'now my eyes have seen you', Job 42:5). Finally, at the end of the story he finishes up blessed twice as richly by God as ever he was before.

We shall never find the complete answer to our question, 'How do we reconcile the suffering in the world with a God of love?' There are pointers to the answer, but in the end we have to trust Him. If we didn't have to trust Him, there would be no need for faith.

CHAPTER 17

# But Doesn't Prayer Work?

Many people today seek to obey Jesus' words when He told His followers to proclaim the kingdom of God, to heal the sick and to drive out unclean spirits. Yet no one nowadays has anywhere near a one hundred per cent success rate in healing. Many were healed through Katharine Kuhlman's ministry. Yet the question which was ever on her lips was, 'Lord, why not all of them?' What has gone wrong when we pray for healing and the person isn't healed?

As I seek to answer that question I put another question: 'Supposing everyone who came to the London Healing Mission was healed – what then?' In no time the media would be on to it. We would be in demand everywhere, both in this country and abroad. The queues for our Healing Services would stretch from Notting Hill Gate to Marble Arch and back again. Those coming here would then come for the healing and not to meet Jesus, whilst we at the Healing Mission would inevitably succumb to the sin of pride. The situation would be self-defeating. It couldn't happen.

Often more people are healed when they come with open hearts to a service of worship than when they come specifically to a 'Healing Service'. If we seek God for what we can give Him, namely ourselves, we begin to get into the relationship with Him which He ordained for mankind in the beginning. Then His power to heal can flow into us. However, if we seek Him for what we can get out of Him, namely the healing, we are not so much loving Him as trying to grasp from Him, and fewer people are healed.

I welcome the increasing emphasis on healing in many churches up and down the country. Yet I still cringe slightly at the announcement of a 'Healing Service'. I would so much rather we referred to them as 'times of worship, at which people get healed'. But sadly that would be too unwieldy a title.

Yet we have certainly seen people healed who were unbelievers, and who then came to know Jesus after receiving their healing.

I am sure the Lord wants to heal more people than we do actually see healed in our churches. What has gone wrong?

I think that probably the most common reason for apparent failure is a lack of perseverance. Jesus told His disciples the story of the widow and the unjust judge (Luke 18) specifically to encourage them to persevere in prayer. Of those people who are healed through prayer, probably only one in every couple of dozen is healed instantaneously (or miraculously). The rest are healed gradually or after a delay. Francis MacNutt (once described as 'the leading authority on healing in the Roman Catholic Church') gives these figures as the experience of many people as well as himself. We would endorse his experience. The greatest mistake one can make, when one prays for somebody to be healed and they are not immediately healed, is to give up and say: 'Oh well, God obviously doesn't want to heal them.' How sad He must be at this lack of perseverance, when He has probably wanted to heal the person all the time!

I sometimes wonder at this apparent change of tactics on our Lord's part, for 2000 years ago it appears that He normally healed instantaneously. We can only guess at the background against which He was working then, but we know that His deepest longing is for each of us to enter into the relationship of love with Him which He planned for us in the beginning. Often it seems that He almost 'trickles out' the healing, a little at a time, in order to encourage us to reach out for more and more of Him.

As we pray, it is important to listen to what Jesus is saying to us through the Holy Spirit. Margaret came to me recently, having had much prayer for healing of M.E. from which, she said, she had suffered for two years and not been healed. Gradually as I prepared myself to pray for her healing I realised that something was wrong. The realisation came to me that I couldn't pray for the Lord to heal her of M.E. Then I realised why.

'You do not have M.E.,' I said to her. I knew nothing about Margaret's family background, but I added: 'Your trouble stems from a wrong relationship with your father many years ago.' Margaret accepted what I said, and I prayed the healing love of Jesus into that wrong relationship.

She came back a week later and, naturally, I rushed up to her, very keen to know whether I had been right in what I had said. 'Yes,' she said. 'The symptoms which were wrongly diagnosed as M.E. have now all gone, since you prayed for my broken relationship with my father.'

Yet though we may wrongly 'hear' the Holy Spirit, the Lord is so good that often He honours us wonderfully when we have stepped out in faith. I remember the man who came to us with terminal cancer. I thought the Lord wanted him to be healed, and I prayed boldly for his healing. Six months later his younger brother came to a service and asked if he could give thanks for answered prayer. His elder brother had died, he said, but on the same evening that we had prayed for him, he had halved the morphine, had given up all his other painkillers, and he had lived twice as long as the doctors had told him was possible. Everyone who had come to visit him had been powerfully blessed by him. I had 'heard' the Holy Spirit wrong, but in His mercy He honoured my stepping out in faith.

Often we forget that God is the God of the whole person, that He longs to perfect His work in us, not just in our bodies, but in our souls and our spirits as well. Sometimes He will, I think, refrain from giving physical healing because He has got something even better for the person. In her book *Joni*, Joni Eareckson describes what she went through as she came to terms with the fact that the Lord was not healing her of the paralysis which still affects the whole of her body from the neck downward, and confines her to a wheelchair. But towards the end of her book, when she has recounted the almost worldwide ministry to other people in wheelchairs which He has opened up for her, she actually says that she is glad He didn't heal her physically, because of the wonderful ministry He has given her through her being in a wheelchair herself. Although there must have been hundreds of people praying for her physical healing, it seems the Lord used those prayers in a different direction, as He prepared her for the ministry she has now. He won't heal us physically if He has something better for us.

But let us remember the situation at Nazareth. On the first occasion Jesus visited His home town after He began His ministry, 'He could not do any miracles.... And he was amazed at their lack of faith' (Mark 6:5–6). We live today in a Nazareth-type situation. Our scientific and materialist culture militates against our being open to the world of the spiritual. A wise old Indian once remarked: 'You in the West have so over-stimulated both the reasoning power of the brain and its retentive power, that you have allowed what should be your normal intuitive power to become atrophied.'

Past hurts can also make it difficult for a person to receive the love and the healing of Jesus in their hearts. The other week Audrey and I were ministering to a lady in her late thirties. I asked her, 'How long did you pray this morning?'

'Two minutes,' she answered.

I went on to ask her how long she had prayed the previous evening and she replied that she had not prayed then.

I was tempted to ask her why on earth she had

come to us for help when she wasn't trying to help herself. Then I realised where the difficulty lay. She had been desperately damaged emotionally in the course of her life. She told us that she had put up barriers to enable her to get through, as one day succeeded another. Those barriers successfully repressed the hurt which was buried deep inside her.

'I can't let Jesus come close to me,' she said. 'If I do, I will have to drop those barriers. I will then go completely to pieces and be unable to hold down my job, let alone live any semblance of normal life.'

As we discussed her problem she accepted that in time the barriers would have to go, for she realised that the only real healing comes from Jesus. It will take much patient and loving ministry but, as the barriers are gradually lowered and as the awful pain of rejection begins to come to the surface, Jesus will heal it bit by bit.

One of the saddest instances was when a woman we will call Jill came to us for healing of depression. She had an adoring husband and two splendid sons and they all waited on her hand and foot. When we prayed for her the Holy Spirit touched her powerfully and it was clear when she came the second time that she was going to be healed, although gradually. But she backed off. If she had been healed, she would have had to take the responsibility of running her own life, and standing on her own feet. In the event, she preferred not to be healed and to continue to have her family waiting on her every whim. Jesus said to the cripple at the Pool of Bethesda, 'Do you want to be healed?'

CHAPTER 18

# Robert Hasn't Been Healed

When we were first asked to write a book about our work here at the London Healing Mission, we put on the back of the book: 'We see the Lord moving in power almost every day at the London Healing Mission.' Many have been the occasions since then when Audrey and I have regretted putting in that word 'almost'! Yet there are times when the Lord does *not* heal.

Robert (not his real name) telephoned me today. We've known Robert for four years and he is a real friend. His problem is multiple sclerosis. We have prayed many times for him, and Robert is completely committed to Jesus. Yet he has not been healed and not only is his M.S. getting worse but he was telling me on the telephone that the pain and the muscular spasms are getting intolerable. He has been given morphine to help deaden the pain but he doesn't want to get hooked on any drug and is trying to take as little as he can.

'What is God doing?' was the cry which came over the telephone. As I listened to him, my heart was bleeding for him. Robert is younger than I am and I found myself thinking: 'What would I feel like, if I were in Robert's position, having really committed my life to the Lord, and yet, apparently, having no answer at all to repeated prayers for healing – indeed, everything seeming to indicate that God wasn't paying any attention to me at all?'

There is no slick answer. How I would have loved to have had an answer which would have solved all Robert's problems. How much more would I have loved to have been able, at my will, to release the Lord's healing power upon him. I found myself thinking of the woman in Bournemouth who came into a meeting where we were speaking. She was supported on either side, but she left unaided, to a burst of clapping. Her problem had been M.S. too. Why hadn't the Lord done something similar for Robert?

I could only tell him that God is a mystery; that God is sovereign; and that there are occasions when He simply hasn't healed.

Robert then told me that he felt he was getting nowhere. At that point, I knew I had something to tell him. I told him of a man whom our son led to the Lord a number of years ago. He used to come regularly to a weekly prayer meeting we had in our own home. I still remember the day, some three months afterwards, when he said to me: 'Andy, I am giving up on this Christianity business. It just doesn't make any difference.' I remember replying to him then: 'My friend, any one of us in this prayer group could tell you, to the day, when you gave your life to the Lord because we have seen Him changing you ever since!' I remember the look of amazement on his face as he looked at me and said, 'Do you really mean that?' and I replied that of course I did.

I was able to tell Robert about that man and I was able moreover to tell him that, even talking to him on the telephone, I was aware of how much he had grown spiritually since we first knew him. This encouraged him, and it was certainly true.

I then remembered a conversation I had had with another friend of ours in a very similar position to Robert. Her problem also is multiple sclerosis, and she has got steadily worse, despite also being a Christian. She, like Robert himself, was confident that, in His own timing, the Lord was going to heal her. But she, like him, was very much aware of an emptiness in her life at the present stage. When we discussed it, it was clear that what each of them meant was that they had no purpose in life. We need to have a purpose in life. 'Where there is no vision, the people perish' (Proverbs 29:18, AV).

I told Robert that the purpose which the Lord had for him at this stage of his life was that he should seek Him with all his heart and grow in His knowledge and His love. I reminded Robert of the words God spoke to David Watson as he was dying of cancer: 'David, I do understand about your ministry, but I want you to understand that My relationship of love with you is even more important!' I told Robert that the most important thing in life, whether one was fit or sick, able-bodied or in a wheelchair, was that wonderful relationship of love with the Lord. Wasn't Robert, after all, going to spend all eternity in utter joy worshipping the Lord? What could make more sense than for him to get on and do just that, right now?

I also suggested to Robert that, if he took as his first objective to grow in that relationship of love with the Lord, his second objective could be to become a really powerful man of prayer.

'Who should I pray for?' Robert asked. 'I hardly see anybody. I am alone in my home. From the time the home help leaves in the middle of the morning to when the nurse comes in the evening, I hardly see anyone.'

I asked him first whether he could see anyone out of the window.

'Yes,' he said, 'I look out on some playing fields. I sometimes see boys playing there.'

'Right,' I said. 'You pray for each one of them. I bet they haven't had anyone praying for them this week! Do you have a television? Do you have a newspaper?'

'Yes,' Robert said, 'I have both.'

I said, 'You turn on the television, you read the newspaper, and you'll find countless people for you to lift up to the Lord in prayer, people who, like the boys in the playing field, probably have had no one to pray for them.'

Thinking back over the conversation, I realised there was one more thing I should have said. However much it seems that circumstances are against us, we need to thank the Lord for what He has given us. It would have helped Robert if I had reminded him to thank God for a comfortable home, for the home help, for the nurse, for the television and the wireless, for enough money, for enough food. I could have gone on and reminded him that, as he thanked the Lord for all He had given him, he could then also pray for those countless other people in the world who had less than he had.

If we are alone too much and, particularly, if we have time on our hands, the danger is that we allow our thoughts to turn inwards to ourselves. That way lie depression and other forms of mental sickness. If we have no purpose in life, we are a sitting target for Satan to feed negative thoughts into our minds. How essential it is for us to accept that, whatever our circumstances, the Lord *does* love us with a love more wonderful than we can ever understand, and to realise that in His love for us He has a real purpose for us and He wants us to grow spiritually each day. (See Mark 12:30–31.)

For centuries the church has known that the redemptive power of the Lord can be released through pain and suffering. No redemptive power is released, however, if we allow the pain we are suffering to dominate our thoughts, still less if we give way to self-pity. If, in the mystery of God's providence, we find ourselves in a situation where we have to endure pain, we need to be resolute about looking away from the pain to the Lord, and worshipping Him, thus using the pain as a kind of stepping-stone to lift us closer to Him. That way we can experience the truth of God's promise: 'In all things God works for the good of those who love him, who have been called according to his purpose' (Romans 8:28).

God is a mystery. But we are told quite clearly in Hebrews 12:5–12, 'My son ... do not lose heart when he rebukes you, because the Lord disciplines those he loves, and he punishes everyone he accepts as a son.... Our fathers disciplined us for a little while as they thought best; but God disciplines us for our good, that we may share in his holiness. No discipline seems pleasant at the time, but painful. Later on, however, it produces a harvest of righteousness and peace for those who have been trained by it. Therefore, strengthen your feeble arms and weak knees!'

CHAPTER 19

# What Does Jesus Feel About Us?

> 'When they came to the home of the synagogue ruler, Jesus saw a commotion, with people crying and wailing loudly. He went in and said to them, "Why all this commotion and wailing? The child is not dead but asleep." But they laughed at him.
>
> After he put them all out, he took the child's father and mother and the disciples who were with him, and went in where the child was. He took her by the hand and said to her, "Talitha koum!" (which means, "Little girl, I say to you, get up!"). Immediately the girl stood up and walked around (she was twelve years old). At this they were completely astonished' (Mark 5:38–42).

It helps us to know Jesus better if we try and understand what must have been in His mind after occasions such as the raising of Jairus' daughter. We do not know what time of day it was when He raised her, but from the context it may well have been in the late afternoon. Jairus and his wife would have invited Jesus to share their evening meal with them and spend the night in their home.

We know there were times when Jesus loved to draw apart and be alone with His heavenly Father, and I expect Jesus slipped out after supper and climbed up the hillside behind the village. Once He had gone high enough to escape the sounds of the village below there would have been a wonderful stillness, broken only by the occasional cry of a bird. Jesus would have sat down on the hillside, while the sun sank low over the Mediterranean Sea.

He would not have been human – and He was completely human besides being the Son of God – if He hadn't let His mind roam back over the events of that busy day. As He sat alone on the hillside He would have experienced again His indignation at seeing the professional mourners bewailing the little girl's supposed death. He would have felt again the hurt of the ridicule they vented against Him when He said she was only asleep. But most important of all, He would have felt again the joy which had been His when He was able to restore the girl to life.

'The reason the Son of God appeared was to destroy the devil's work' (1 John 3:8), and Jesus knew that in snatching the girl from death to life He was pushing back the boundaries of Satan's kingdom. He had once again done that for which He had come into this world. There would have been joy in His heart as He relived in His memory the excitement when He handed the girl, alive and well, to her parents. As He sat there reliving the occasion, He would have lifted his eyes to heaven and the joy in His heart would have been echoed in the heart of His Father.

By now the sun would be sinking down and Jesus would have got up and begun to pick His way down the hill, towards the home where He was to pass the night.

As He went down His heart would have been filled with eager anticipation. Tomorrow was going to be the first time since His ministry began when He would be going to His own home town. We remember how Luke tells us that after the temptation in the wilderness Jesus returned 'in the power of the Spirit' (Luke 4:14) and for the first time He would now be going back to Nazareth in His ministry of power.

He would, perhaps, have thought of the boy, a contemporary of His, who had been dropped by his mother as a baby. It was one of those accidents, but the boy had been crippled ever since. How wonderful it would be tomorrow when He laid His hands on him and set him free to walk properly for the first time in his life.

He might have thought, too, of the girl, a little older than Himself, who had been born blind. How wonderful to heal her tomorrow so that she could see her husband and children for the first time.

His mind might have gone to the friend of His who, He had heard on the grapevine, had become a leper. He would be sheltering in some cave near Nazareth, cast out from his home, and living on scraps of food people threw at him. How wonderful to think of healing him and restoring him to his family and friends.

Thus it must have been with a keen sense of anticipation of what was to follow tomorrow that

Jesus slipped quietly into the house and lay down to sleep.

But let us allow Mark to continue the story.

> 'Jesus left there and went to his home town, accompanied by his disciples. When the Sabbath came, he began to teach in the synagogue.... Jesus said to them, "Only in his home town, among his relatives and in his own house is a prophet without honour." He could not do any miracles there, except lay his hands on a few sick people and heal them. And he was amazed at their lack of faith' (Mark 6:1–6).

Once again we can imagine Jesus excusing Himself that evening after supper in one of the homes in Nazareth. It would have been with a heavy heart that He climbed one of the neighbouring hills, longing to be alone and away from the distractions of men.

As He sat down on the hillside, once again His mind would have gone back to the events of the day. He had seen the man who was crippled since being dropped as a baby – and he was still crippled. The woman who was blind was still unable to see her husband and her children. He hadn't seen the leper but He knew that his condition was unchanged and he was still a lonely outcast sheltering in some cave.

Mark tells us that all He had been able to do was lay His hands on a few sick people and heal them. Perhaps they had had a stomach upset or a touch of flu. He had been unable to do any miracles because of their unbelief. Again He marvelled within Himself at their lack of faith.

There must have been great sadness in Jesus' heart as He thought of all those in His own home town whom He had been longing to heal with His miracles – and they were still unchanged. How His heart would have gone out to them as He sat on that lonely hillside knowing what He might have done for them had He found faith in that little village. As He looked up to heaven how the disappointment and the sadness in His heart would have been echoed in the heart of His heavenly Father.

It is as we reflect on what must have been in Jesus' mind on some of the occasions in the Gospel stories that we get to know Him better. But we need to go further and remember that Jesus Christ is the same yesterday and today and for ever (Hebrews 13:8). There will be the same delight and elation in Jesus' heart today in heaven, when we who are faithful to Him perform some work of power, drawing on His Holy Spirit. On the other hand, there will be the same sense of disappointment when He longs to see one of His loved ones comforted and healed at our hands, and He again marvels at our lack of faith when nothing happens. As we reflect on what goes on in our own church or fellowship, we may find ourselves wondering, as day follows day, which feeling dominates in His heart – a feeling of delight as He sees us doing His work, or a feeling of sadness when through lack of faith no mighty works are done.

We need to ask ourselves that question. The answer when it comes can be uncomfortable.

CHAPTER 20

# On Loving Myself

I'm always thankful for Jesus' words when He said that He would send the Holy Spirit, and the Holy Spirit would lead us into all truth. As we seek to follow the Lord in this life, gradually the Holy Spirit unfolds more and more of His truth for us. For a long time I had difficulty with Jesus' words when He told us to love our neighbours *as ourselves*. What did this mean? Surely it sounded like an invitation to be self-centred and selfish?

Let's see what His words do not mean. Mum takes the kids down to the sea on a sunny day. She buys little Johnnie a chocolate ice-cream. Johnnie says he wants another. Mum says: 'All right, just one more.'

Johnnie guzzles that one down. 'Mum, I want another!'

Mum says, 'No.' But Johnnie starts screaming, so to keep the peace she buys him one more. Johnnie guzzles that one down, too.

'I want another!' he shouts. 'I want! I want! I want!'

This is not Johnnie loving himself. This is plain selfishness. To give in to selfishness is bad for us.

Loving ourselves must be good for us, or else Jesus wouldn't have told us to do it.

What does it mean? I think first we must realise the interlocking nature of the two commandments which Jesus quoted from the Old Testament to sum up the whole of the teaching of the previous 1500 years. First and foremost comes the commandment to love God with everything we've got – the God with whom Jesus identified Himself so completely. There follows on from that commandment the double commandment, to love our neighbours as ourselves. I don't believe it is possible for us to love our neighbours unless we do love ourselves.

George (not his real name) came to see me one day. He's a solicitor of about sixty. He had written telling me of his problems which he described as feelings of rejection followed by hatred and anger. He went on to say that he always expected to be rejected, and always was. He felt a failure.

As we are ministering here, we are always trying to listen with our third ear to what the Lord is saying. I took a chance. 'Would you understand what I meant,' I said, 'if I suggested that deep down within you there is a little George and that he is full of fear and is hurting deeply?'

I was relieved when George said 'Yes' to both points. He understood that there was the little boy deep inside him, and he accepted that the root of the problem was that that little boy was scared stiff, and hurting.

I then tried to tell him about loving himself. 'There is the big George,' I said, 'the big George who is in your head, and there is the little George, deep, deep down inside you who is hiding away in away in fear.' I went on to tell him to minister the love of Jesus from himself, the big George, to the little George inside him.

I explained that, although we are in control of our minds (we can stop thinking about something and think of something else at will), we are not in control of our unconscious. If we try to coerce, or bully, our unconscious minds, in other words, the 'little me' that is deep within us, the 'little me' simply gets more frightened and hides deeper. We can, however, make contact with the little one inside us if we approach him with kindness, gentleness and love.

I told George to spend a quarter of an hour, morning and evening, loving himself, that is loving the little George inside him. 'Explain to him that he need not be afraid any longer,' I said. 'Encourage him to come out of his hiding place into the light. Tell him you love him, that you value him and invite him to come up from the depths where he is hiding and to hold your hand and talk to you.'

When the little George is encouraged with gentleness and love to come up and join the big George, then George will be integrated and he will be a whole person. If the two parts are jarring, and the 'big me' is riding rough-shod over the 'little me', then we will never have the peace of God. Harmful consequences will follow in every area of life, body and mind and spirit.

Elizabeth has been coming to see Audrey and me every month or so for half-a-dozen months now. She had been much rejected by her mother in childhood and then again by her foster parents. She had then married a man who, quite frankly, was inadequate. The way he had sought to bolster up his self-confidence was by putting her down. He had put her down and, indeed, trampled on her, for the last thirty-five years.

For the last twenty-five years Elizabeth has been in real pain. The pain has come in different parts of her body, her head, her neck, her shoulders, and her back, and it has defied all the efforts of the doctors. Some months ago we suggested to Elizabeth that she wanted to hold on to the pain.

Elizabeth exploded! 'Whatever do you think I'm coming here for, if it isn't to get rid of the pain!' she said quite heatedly. 'Of course I want to get rid of the pain!'

It was a month or two later that we began to see what the problem was. We told her about the 'little Elizabeth' deep within her heart. 'The little Elizabeth,' we said to her, 'has been screaming out for love all your life. Because you haven't been paying any attention to her, she has put this pain on you.' It is quite possible for things which are wrong in our unconscious minds to bring about pain which doctors sometimes call psychosomatic. We told her that we didn't believe the root of the problem lay in the pain itself. We told her how to minister the love of Jesus to the little Elizabeth. In brief, we told her how to love herself. I think we have seen her a couple of times since then and she tells us that the physical pain is gradually beginning to go.

Let me tell you, then, about Beatrice. Beatrice is no single real person, but an amalgam of three separate people I've ministered to in the last fortnight. Each of them has suffered great rejection and much pain from early childhood. They use words like these: 'I go round constantly carrying a big placard. The placard reads in large letters: "Keep your distance! I can't bear to let you come close to me!"' Again, this is one of the reactions which may follow from childhood hurt, but these defences also keep out love. Moreover, it is only love which will melt down these defences.

The answer has been for Beatrice to understand the little Beatrice deep within her and to love the little Beatrice. Then, with the gentle encouragement of love, the little Beatrice will come to drop her placard. As the big Beatrice and the little Beatrice come together, and as the placard is no longer needed, it will become quite natural for Beatrice to love those around her who are her neighbours.

It all starts with the two-way relationship of love which needs to be set free to flow between the Lord and ourselves. As we receive His love for ourselves and as, in return, we love Him, we can then minister His love to the little one which is deep down within us. Then, as we learn to love ourselves, we can love our neighbours.

Thus we obey the whole of the Old Testament law, all of which was summed up in those two great commandments which Jesus gave us. He said: '"Love the Lord your God with all your heart and with all your soul and with all your mind." This is the first and greatest commandment. And the second is like it: "Love your neighbour as yourself"' (Matthew 22:37–39).

CHAPTER 21

# On Touching Jesus

Although many of us live in large and crowded cities, we are often curiously reluctant to touch each other. Often we find it difficult to understand how simpler people, living 2000 years ago, felt it natural to touch someone and to hold on to them. We see instances of this in Jesus' resurrection appearances.

Matthew tells us how the women hurried away from Jesus' tomb, running to tell His disciples what an angel had told them. Then suddenly Jesus met them and greeted them. Matthew continues: 'They came to him, clasped his feet and worshipped him' (Matthew 28:9). It came naturally to them to touch Jesus and to hold Him.

As we consider that occasion, it is hard for us to comprehend the surge of emotions which must have come tumbling from the hearts of that group of women as they saw Jesus once again. Indeed, we cannot understand what they must have felt unless we realise something of the utter despair they would have been feeling from the time of His crucifixion up to that very moment.

Those women had accompanied Jesus during the time of His ministry. They had staked everything on their belief that He really was the long-awaited Messiah, the Son of God, and that somehow – they knew not how – He was going to bring redemption to their people.

Then when they saw Him crucified they must, indeed, have felt that the very bottom had fallen out of their world. Instead of victory for the man they had followed and loved, here, it seemed, was total and ignominious defeat. Jesus had failed. So it must have appeared to them. It is impossible for us to realise the depth of despair and disillusionment which must have filled their hearts.

Then came the astounding message of the angel. Their natural instinct was to run and tell the disciples what he had said to them. Yet, as they ran, and as the import of the angel's words began to sink into them, they must have felt that they just didn't dare to believe what he had told them. It would just be too wonderful if Jesus really was alive again, but they couldn't bear to face the possibility of there having been some mistake on the angel's part. What if, after all, they were still to be faced with blank disillusionment and despair?

Then they saw Jesus. They saw the familiar figure. They heard His familiar words of greeting. It was true! Here was Jesus – the man they had loved so dearly and followed so faithfully – alive and well before them. We can only guess at the joy which was bursting forth from their hearts as they greeted Him.

They threw themselves to the ground before Him and tumbled over each other, seeking, each of them, to clasp His feet in worship and adoration.

At that supreme moment in their lives it came naturally to them to hold Him.

Meanwhile, what was going on in Jesus' mind? He had suffered grievously during His life on earth. In His heart there must still have been the thankfulness with which He had uttered His last great cry from the cross: 'It is finished' (John 19:30). When He had uttered those words He had known that the purpose for which He had come into this world had been completed and He was free to dismiss His spirit.

That cry had been a cry of triumph and that feeling of triumph must still have been in Jesus' mind as the women rushed to greet Him. At the same time there must have been in His heart the joy of being reunited with those whom He loved deeply. Jesus welcomed them holding His feet.

I think Jesus always welcomed people touching Him. We read in Luke 24:39 that Jesus said to His disciples: 'It is I myself! Touch me and see.'

Then, on a later occasion, when Thomas was present, Jesus addressed him: 'Put your finger here.... Reach out your hand and put it into my side' (John 20:27).

It is true that only ten verses earlier Jesus is reported as having said to Mary Magdalene: 'Do not hold on to me, for I have not yet returned to the Father' (John 20:17). These reported words seem inconsistent with the other records. It is worth commenting, however, that if an early copyist had made a mistake of only one letter in the Greek word which is translated 'hold', the words would read, 'Do not be afraid.' There would then be no inconsistency.

With this one possible exception, it does seem

With this one possible exception, it does seem beyond doubt that Jesus welcomed being touched and, indeed, handled by His followers. When St John is at pains, in the beginning of his first letter, to make clear that Jesus really had been with them as a man of flesh and blood, he declares that his very own hands had touched Him.

Jesus is still the same. Some years ago, I was praying with a woman of around fifty who had had a desperately unhappy married life and had suffered much. As usual here, we stood to pray and I must have been praying with her for fifteen minutes or so.

When I finished she turned round and thanked me, adding: 'Thank you so much, too, for holding my hand while you were praying.'

'But I never touched you,' I said. She said she had clearly felt someone holding her right hand with quite a firm grip as I prayed with her.

We agreed that it could only have been Jesus. It meant an enormous lot to that sad and damaged woman that Jesus had wanted to touch her and to hold her hand.

Not long ago Audrey and I were praying with a girl who, for various reasons, had no emotions. She said it was as if there was a barrier of stone across her chest.

One evening we spent nearly two hours praying with her. Towards the end she began to be aware that the stone barrier was beginning to loosen. At the end she turned round and said to us: 'As you were praying, for the first time in my life I was able to see Jesus. As I looked (and as you continued to pray) Jesus came up to me. He touched my chest with His hand and He told me that it would be all right.'

The other night the Lord showed me something new in my prayer life. Sometimes when I pray I see Him as light. Sometimes I see Him as a young man. There are times when I see Him as quite a young boy – and I remember Isaiah's words that 'a little child will lead them'.

The Lord woke me up that night, about three o'clock in the morning, to pray. On that occasion I was vividly aware of Him as a little boy aged, perhaps, ten or eleven. But as I enjoyed the wonder of being with Him, I found myself thinking, 'This is not enough; there must be something more.' As I prayed I found myself moving forward until I didn't just touch Him, but I held Him. I clasped Him.

For me that experience has opened up a new dimension of prayer. I now believe that we are not only to try and use the sense of sight as we seek to visualise Him in our prayers, but that we are also meant to use the sense of touch and, as we enjoy being with Him, to reach out and hold Him.

It is indeed true that Jesus is the same yesterday and today and for ever (Hebrews 13:8). As we have seen, when He was a man on earth, Jesus loved His friends to hold Him and, indeed, to fondle Him – to use their sense of touch as a further means of contact with Him.

I believe He wants the same today. I believe, too, that as we seek to relive with Mary Magdalene the wonder of being reunited with Jesus that Easter morning, so we can reach out in prayer and clasp Him.

CHAPTER 22

# 'I Can't Help Worrying'

Let's call her Anne. She was a woman of about fifty who came up for prayer at the end of one of our Healing Services. 'Life is so stressful,' she said. As we talked it was clear that she was a lovely Christian, that she knew the Lord and she loved Him, but her problem was that she couldn't stop worrying. Her worrying had become so much part of her that she couldn't see how she could ever get free, though she longed to. (Yet she still wondered, rather apprehensively, what would be left of her if she were to be set free!)

If we let ourselves get into the way of worrying, it will lead to an inner tension. That tension or stress can in its turn lead to many forms of sickness – migraines, headaches, digestive troubles and even heart trouble. Many doctors say that half the sicknesses today – some doctors say well over half – are caused or, at the least, are made worse by this stress.

Anne wanted to be set free from her ingrained habit of worrying, worrying about anything, even worrying, at times, about nothing. As one of her children had often said to her: 'If you hadn't got anything to worry about, you'd go on worrying until you found something to worry about!'

It is always much easier to pray *for* something rather than to pray against something. It is easier to reach out and pray for the positive thing rather than to pray against the negative thing. I asked Anne what she felt was the opposite of worry, and she replied: 'Love'. People give different answers to that question. Sometimes they say: 'Peace'. For myself, it seems that the opposite of worry is to have a childlike trust in Jesus – after all, if you have that trust you just can't worry. 'Perfect love drives out fear' (1 John 4:18), and worry is a form of fear – fear of the unknown, fear of what might happen, or fear of what might not happen.

We prayed quite briefly with Anne, taking the sword of the Holy Spirit and cutting her free from the bondage to worry which she had got herself into. There can be a real release of spiritual power as one seeks to break such a habit in the name of Jesus.

But however dramatic the spiritual experience of such a prayer may sometimes be, Satan will almost always try to counter-attack. Many of us are familiar with the sneering voice which says: 'You don't really expect anything to have changed, do you? All right, you had a bit of a spiritual high at that service. But you're an intelligent person, and you know that that didn't make any real difference, don't you?'

We told Anne, therefore, that she must do her part to ensure that she stayed free from the habit of worrying. We therefore prayed with her that the Lord would fill her with His love and that she would come to trust Him with a childlike trust.

We thus helped her to pray for the positive thing, having set her free from the negative thing.

We went further: 'You realise, don't you,' we said, 'that Jesus has heard that prayer? You accept, don't you, that that prayer was in line with the will of the Lord?' Anne seemed to hesitate for a moment. 'Surely you can see,' we said, 'that the worry which disturbs your peace of mind is a destructive thing and must therefore be from Satan, whereas it must be the will of a God of perfect love that you be filled with a loving childlike trust in Him.'

Anne agreed. We told her then to thank Him that He had heard her prayer. We reminded her that the Lord always answers prayer when we are praying in line with His perfect will for the situation which we are praying about (1 John 5:14).

'Thank Him,' we said. 'Keep on thanking Him that He is in fact giving you more and more of His love and His peace. Keep on thanking Him that gradually, even though perhaps imperceptibly, He's beginning to develop in you a lovely childlike trust in Him. Remember, we can't love Him unless we trust Him, and Jesus said that loving Him is the most important thing in our lives.'

But in a situation like Anne's, the temptation to give in to worry can sweep over one unexpectedly and from nowhere. It can seem to overwhelm one and to take one completely by surprise. We told her that if she found herself almost compelled to start worrying over something again, she must take the decision with her will to turn to Jesus and praise Him. If she had the gift of tongues we would have told her to turn to Him and praise Him in tongues. But she hadn't (yet?) received this gift. We told her, therefore, as soon as the worrying seemed about to overwhelm her, to turn to Jesus and quite resolutely to thank Him that He was giving her His love, His peace and that lovely childlike trust in Him.

We need to remember that Satan often works through echoes. We all know what an echo is. If we hear an echo it sounds exactly like the real thing, but we know that there's nothing there, just emptiness. We told Anne that if she felt the temptation to worry suddenly sweeping over her she must recognise that it was only an echo and therefore without substance. There would be no power in it, and in the strength of Jesus she would be able to turn away from the feeling of worry and to fill her heart with thankfulness to Him that He was, indeed, giving her His peace and His love.

She wouldn't feel like saying it, the words would be quite mechanical, but we explained to her that that prayer must be true because Jesus *had* heard our prayer, and it *was* in line with His will.

She could therefore pray it, albeit without any feelings, yet without any fear of being hypocritical.

Thus is Satan defeated. Thus we can draw on the power of the Holy Spirit within us to set us free.

CHAPTER 23

# Tolerance? Or Speak Out?

When is it right for the Christian to speak out openly against what is wrong? And when does the Holy Spirit guide us simply to express Christian love? I believe this is a problem which many of us need to face, as we seek to follow Jesus. I believe, too, it is an area where much harm can be done. We have seen this in the lives of those people who come to us hurt and damaged by overzealous 'shepherding' in some of the house churches.

But all of us must have welcomed the initiatives taken unceasingly over the last twenty years by Mary Whitehouse. She has fought and fought again to restrain the worst excesses of sexual 'freedom' in the media. Similarly, Clifford Hill speaks out in *Prophecy Today* against the deception of the New Age movement, a movement which teaches the self-sufficiency of man and denies our need for Jesus.

Again, Audrey and I were heartened to read recently that Cardinal Basil Hume had spoken out against Parliament's 'appalling' decisions on embryo experimentation and abortion. He said, 'We have dispensed with the traditional Christian vision of the sanctity of human life.... There is an urgent need for our society to rediscover the respect and dignity belonging to all human life, young or old, whether handicapped or not.' Thank God, we say, for people of courage who stand up and speak out for what is right.

Indeed, much could be written about the sin of tolerance in our society today. In her book *Life in a Sex-Mad Society*, Joyce Huggett criticises the widely-held view, 'If it's going to give me pleasure and if it's not hurting anybody, why not go ahead and do it?' More than ever one sees the need for certain absolute standards of right and wrong. Cardinal Hume recognised that his views were in a minority but he added that he had the right to express what he believed to be the truth. Would that more people would do the same.

Yet I believe we need to be particularly sensitive to the Holy Spirit's guidance. Audrey and I have increasingly come to see that in our one-to-one ministry here at the Mission it is usually wrong to knock the other person's views. Let me give several examples.

A Muslim woman came to see Audrey a few weeks ago. It would have been very easy for Audrey to have quoted Muhammad's denial that Jesus actually died on the cross. Muhammad claimed that He only swooned, that He then came to, in the cool of the tomb, and that He lived on for many years after. (If that were true, it would cut at the very basis of the doctrine of atonement.) She could have quoted Muhammad's own teaching that in this life men could have up to four wives (he actually had eleven himself), and that if his followers died waging war on the infidel they would go straight to Paradise to be entertained with an endless number of young ladies.

But Audrey tells me that she never said anything against the faith of the woman who had come to see her. She merely tried to show her Jesus – and the woman left a Christian.

I had the same experience myself with someone who came to me as a Zen Buddhist and with other non-Christian ideas. I never spoke against that person's beliefs, but that person today is a wonderfully committed Christian, totally dedicated to seeking more and more of the knowledge and love of Jesus.

Perhaps it was the same reasoning which coloured our approach to Freemasonry in the pamphlet we have produced, and which was quoted in the report on Freemasonry to the General Synod of the Church of England. I have read articles by Christians on Freemasonry asserting that it is Satanic and that, in the end, it leads to the worship of Satan. (At this stage I am not saying whether or not that statement is true!) But it is a fact that there are many good, decent people, often churchgoers, who are also Freemasons. To express such a view would only antagonise them. In our pamphlet, instead of knocking Freemasonry, we try and draw the reader's attention to what Christianity has to offer.

We must always remember that the Lord loves the other person, whatever his or her views, every bit as much as He loves us. We must always remember that none of us is worthy of His love.

We must always remember that the divine miracle is that nonetheless He loves each one of us imperfect human beings. 'All have sinned and fall short of the glory of God' (Romans 3:23).

Yet even in one-to-one ministry there are times when one has to challenge people. A mother brought her sixteen-year-old daughter to me recently. The girl was convinced that she had cut herself off from the forgiveness and the love of God. She was convinced that she was going to go to hell, and would burn there for all eternity. I talked to her at length about the love of Jesus, His forgiveness and His wonderful victory on the cross over the powers of darkness, into whose grip she had let herself slip. But the time came when I had to present her with the choice. 'The path you are on is leading you to torment, darkness and, ultimately, to destruction,' I said. 'You have the choice to turn the other way. That other way leads to light, to joy, to Jesus, and to eternal life.'

She had still not uttered a single word to me, so repressed was she. At this point I said that I could spend no more time with her, the decision was now up to her. I would see her again at lunchtime if she, of her own choice, decided to turn to Jesus and to accept His forgiveness, His love and His life.

I was so afraid that she would not come back. But she did. I am sure there was great rejoicing in heaven.

How can one sum up these thoughts? One can only say that in this, as in every other area of our lives, there is the need to listen in all humility to what the Lord is saying to us through His Holy

Spirit. If we will still our hearts and gaze on Him in love and adoration we can be sure that, in the stillness of His presence, He will guide us.

CHAPTER 24

# 'L' Plates

When my wife Audrey and I first came to the London Healing Mission, we had seen two or three people healed through prayer but there was no question of our then having a 'healing ministry' ourselves. Indeed I would have gladly dropped through the floor when I went to be interviewed by the Trustees and heard the senior Trustee declare, 'This is the man God has chosen to head up the London Healing Mission.' For her part Audrey was on record as having said that the Mission was the last place in the world she would ever go to!

Yet, as we have written in an earlier book, the Lord had made it clear to us, and He confirmed it, and confirmed it again, that we were to take over the London Healing Mission. So there we were in the early days of April 1983, duly installed. People were already booking appointments to see us, they were coming to the chapel services, and we still felt we had no healing ministry. 'God *must* have common sense,' we assured each other. 'If God has chosen to send us here to run the Mission, it must follow that He will show us what to do.' We had no choice but to put our trust in the Lord. How wonderfully He has honoured that! (It was less than a year afterwards that a firm of publishers wrote asking us to write a book describing our work at the Mission!)

In fact, as the years have gone by, we have come to see that it was an advantage going to the Mission with no previous experience. We had no choice but to cast ourselves on the mercy of God at every turn. Every time somebody walked in to keep an appointment, we could only pray, 'Lord, You will just have to show us.' It seemed that He was training us to rely completely on Him and not to rely on ourselves.

The story has gone on in the same way ever since. Last June we went up to a well-known Christian centre to see if we could learn from them. Forty-eight hours later they were asking us to take on someone who had been deeply into witchcraft for many years, and whom they felt they couldn't take on. As we have ministered to her the Lord has continued to teach us, as indeed has been the case with many others to whom we have ministered. All the time as we find our ministry developing, we know that we are leaning on Him and looking to Him to guide us, so that He may use us ever more fully.

One of our team consulted me some years ago about doing a course in counselling. I told her I was quite happy for her to do the course, but I warned her that if she did the course, the risk was that when she was presented with someone with an unusual problem, she would think back to what she had been taught on her course, rather than throwing herself on His mercy, and crying out, 'Lord, show me.' She did in fact take the course, but I felt the warning had been needed.

When we first came to the Mission, Audrey and I were running it ourselves, with one girl, part-time. With the growth of the work, we now have a team of some twenty-five people. Some of them only work part-time, but usually we have ten people present at the Mission each day. Sometimes people ask us, 'How do you train them?'

The training is 'on the job'. We start them off in the general office, where the telephone ministry takes place, and with two or three people always in that office they learn from each other as they hear each other ministering over the phone; they have the opportunity of discussing telephone calls amongst themselves (though always respecting the confidentiality of the caller).

In addition we have a time of sharing Holy Communion at the beginning of each day. Lunching together, as we always do, gives a further opportunity of discussion. But before we let people minister on their own, they minister jointly for a time with one of the team who is more experienced.

Some years ago a girl joined us who was rather retiring and shy. Her very first morning she took a call and the woman on the other end said, 'Would you please pray for the healing of my eye? I have an abscess.' The girl swallowed hard, then launched out boldly in prayer. Half an hour later, the woman rang back to say that the abscess was already going. If we throw ourselves on His mercy, He honours what we have done.

I always feel that if one of the team were to come to us and say, 'We know what to do here,' we would very gently but firmly show them the door! We want people here who realise their need to lean on the Lord and listen to what He is saying. When we humble ourselves before Him and lean on Him, how He does indeed honour our stepping out in faith. The work continues to grow. We never advertise either our counselling or the Healing Services in the chapel. People come only from personal recommendation, and more and more seem to come.

But we are well aware of the vital importance of being humble before the Lord. I put a red 'L' plate in the general office under the words 'London Healing Mission logo', and lest I ever forget the need to humble myself before the Lord, I have another one in front of me on my desk.

Recently Audrey and I were having supper with Bishop Morris Maddocks and his wife Anne. 'Don't ever lose your humility before God,' Morris said to us. We know full well that if we ever lost it the power would go out of our ministry.

Often if two or more of us are ministering together, it seems as if the Lord deliberately arranges matters so that each of us only contributes a part, and neither of us can take credit for the guidance He reveals to us or for the healing which follows. He knows our weakness as human beings, and He wants us to remain humble before Him. He wants us always to give Him all the glory. Often at the Mission we feel that we just stand back, our mouths open with wonder, as we see the Lord moving in His power.

It was this thought which led us to start having a monthly teaching day. We so long to see more and more churches and fellowships experiencing the living Lord in the way we experience Him at the Mission. The teaching days have always been fully booked.

In the same way, we often do teaching weekends, whether in England or overseas. The motive is always the same: we long to see more and more people entering into a deeper and more wonderful knowledge of Jesus, and we dearly want them to experience His reality in their lives, so that they too may say, 'We see Him moving in power almost every day.'

I think humility before Jesus and obedience to Him are the two keys. The more we continue in our ministry, the more we find ourselves saying with John the Baptist, 'He must become greater and greater, and I must become less and less' (John 3:30, Living Bible). Our 'L' plates will be in place as long as we are at the Mission.

CHAPTER 25

# Be Practical

Someone once said: 'What's the use of being so heavenly-minded that you're no earthly use?' I used to dismiss this as a cynical remark, but there is wisdom in it.

As Christians, we are meant to be in the world and we are meant to be radiating the love of Jesus to those with whom we come in contact. Someone once pictured a Christian as an old-fashioned miller covered with flour making his way through a crowd: he left a bit of white on everybody he brushed up against. If we are not radiating the love of Jesus to those around us and if we are not bringing in any harvest for Him, then indeed we are not fulfilling His work in the world. In that case, such 'heavenly-mindedness' as we may have will be false. If we love the Lord and if we are in His will, then we will be bearing fruit for Him during our walk through this life.

As we think further, we see that however 'spiritual' a man or woman may be, if they are really in the Lord's will, they are also practical. James reminds us of this when he writes: 'What's the use of saying that you ... are Christians if you aren't proving it by helping others.... If you have a friend who is in need of food and clothing, and you say to him, "Well, goodbye and God bless you; stay warm and eat up," and then don't give him clothes or food, what good does that do?' (James 2:14–16, Living Bible). In the same way, when Paul wrote to Timothy, the young man who meant so much to him and who was often ill, he advised him to take a little wine sometimes for the benefit of his stomach (1 Timothy 5:23).

It's very easy here at the Healing Mission to let one's advice be limited to what is spiritual. I was reminded the other day of the need to be practical as well, when we received a telephone call from a thirty-year-old man who had spent many years in and out of mental hospitals. Twice in the recent weeks he had fallen away from Jesus, and twice he had responded to my challenge, confessed his slipping away and committed himself afresh to the Lord. But then, the day after we had last talked, he telephoned me. 'What has gone wrong?' he asked me. 'I really am praying, I really am reading the Bible, and yet I can't cope. Is it my lack of faith, or is something else wrong?' I realised that, whilst I had been right to get him to repent of his falling away, and to lead him to giving his life afresh to Jesus, I had left it at that, without covering the practical issues. I hadn't told him how to live out that total commitment of himself to Jesus.

The young man's predicament was one which is all too common nowadays; he lives alone and has much too much time on his hands, as he is unemployed. How does one counsel people like that, so that they may live their lives productively and to the glory of God? Having too much time and too little company can, indeed, be a devastating combination for so many of us.

Remembering Jesus' instructions on how we should live our lives, namely that we should love God with everything we have, I told him of the importance not only of having a set time each day when he would begin his time of prayer, but also of having a set time for finishing. Praying reflects our commitment to this command to love the Lord our God, which Jesus described as the first and greatest commandment. As well as having a set time of prayer, we need to get into the way of being aware of His presence right through the day, and, if we are alone a lot, of sharing every thought with Him.

We come, then, to the second of Jesus' two great commandments, 'Love your neighbour as yourself.' My mind goes back to an elderly spinster who died some years ago. She had an exquisite flat, beautifully panelled, with lovely pictures, china and ornaments. She had, moreover, two spare bedrooms. I often thought how sad it was that, in her pride for her beautiful flat, she felt she couldn't share it with someone else. Or perhaps it wasn't pride, but was fear of having someone intruding on her privacy? Either way, I couldn't help feeling that, if she had taken the plunge and invited a couple of young Christian girls to make their home with her, she would have suffered much less from the loneliness which plagued her during the closing years of her life.

Then, by way of contrast, I think of a girl who came to see me a few days ago. She had had a very unhappy childhood and, as a result, had been unable to enter into a stable relationship with a man. She had married young, soon been divorced, married again, been divorced again, and then had a succession of lovers. Then, at the age of thirty-four, the wholly unexpected happened and she became a Christian. She was unemployed, and I asked her how she spent her time; it was clear that she was totally committed to the Lord and she said her problem was seeing everyone she wanted to see during the day. It is indeed true, as she has proved herself, that if we are totally available to the Lord, He will bring people to us so that we can minister His love and His healing to them. Already, the Lord was using her powerfully in His service; we just need to make ourselves available. She was putting into practice Jesus' words to us all: 'Love your neighbour as yourself.'

I think, then, of the elderly lady who was living alone and was confined through ill health to her flat. How was it possible for her to glorify God in her very restricted life? Whilst she could certainly express her love for the Lord in prayer, how could her life bear fruit in giving love to her neighbour? Her flat looked out over a street, and I suggested that one answer for her was to time herself for an hour a day, looking out through the window at the individual people as they passed on the pavement. I told her that if she looked into their faces as they went by, she would see so much to pray for. A business man would pass by and she could lift him up in prayer to the Lord, praying that his eyes might be opened to see the Lord's will. A woman might come by, looking tense and anxious, and she could pray that the

Lord would give her His peace. A boy and a girl might pass by, arm in arm, and she could pray that the Lord might keep His hand on the two of them in their relationship.

I can't remember if that old lady was able to get out to church, but when we go to our church or fellowship we need to look around for the often unattractive person who is standing alone, shy and self-conscious; that is the person Jesus would have spoken to. If we can bring ourselves to ask that person round for a cup of coffee, once he or she has gained confidence in us, we shall find that underneath a perhaps rather unattractive exterior there is a warm heart. We find again that 'it is in blessing that we ourselves are blessed'.

Perhaps the most practical advice for someone who is alone a lot and who has too much time to spare is to buy an alarm clock. All of us need to organise our days; we need to have a time out in the fresh air taking exercise, we need to keep ourselves clean and tidy, we need to eat properly at meal times and not have snacks in between. All this does, actually, give glory to God.

But this implies that we have sufficient strength of character to discipline ourselves. Lately, I have been trying to help a man of twenty-six who is so caught up in himself that, all the time he is talking to me (or to anyone else), he is looking down at the floor with his head in his hands; his hair looks as though it hasn't been brushed for a month and I am certain that he hasn't changed his shirt from the day I first saw him. How can one expect a man like that to plan his day?

I am trying to help that man to gain confidence in himself and to build up his self-respect, but it is a long haul. Really what he needs is not to be found at the London Healing Mission. What he needs is some neighbour who will give him the combination of kindness and firmness which he needs; criticism would be the reverse of helpful. He needs someone with patience who can see that Jesus loves him as much as He loves other people.

He is the man Jesus would have sought out. So when you go to your church, will you please look out for that man? It helps neither God nor man if we're so heavenly-minded that we're no earthly use.

CHAPTER 26

# Of Time and Eternity

When I was in my mid-forties I realised that God was saying He wanted me in the ordained ministry. I remember sharing this with our elderly neighbour. 'I have a feeling,' I added, 'that quite often men in their mid-forties may rethink their basic attitudes to life, to religion and to God.'

'That's nothing!' came my neighbour's quick reply. 'You wait till you're in your mid-eighties. Then you really *will* rethink what you believe!'

Lately I've been realising how false my time-scale has often been. When we are growing up, it seems that life in this world is almost infinite. As we contemplate, in our teens, having perhaps seventy or even eighty more years ahead of us, it seems like an eternity. We are tempted to believe that anything beyond that just isn't worth thinking about.

Then we get into a job and, unconsciously, as the years go by, we think in terms of working until retirement age. Life becomes a matter of coping with the working years – and again, it seems that what comes after retirement can be left till the time comes. 'Each day has enough trouble of its own,' we say to ourselves (Matthew

6:34) – forgetting that Satan, too, is adept at quoting scripture!

Now that I'm in my sixties and well into my second career, the Lord has been showing me that the time ahead of me really is infinite! I am beginning to take in that there is to be no retirement from my present 'career' (that is, if my 'career' can now be defined as making myself available to serve the Lord wherever and however He wants me to). There is to be no time ahead when I sit back and do what I think I would like to do, while I gradually lapse into old age. Instead there is to be a continual 'pressing on' to know the Lord more clearly, there is to be the ever-increasing joy of trusting myself to Him more and more completely, and there is to be the ever more wonderful fulfilment of worshipping Him and serving Him.

And now there is no time-scale! Death will be but an incident on the way. In Winston Churchill's words, death is only 'the end of the beginning'. After death it will be the same as before, only very much more so! We cannot see clearly what life will be like when we are in eternity. There will be no past and no future since there will be no time. But there will be a glorious unending present of perfect joy.

No wonder Paul wrote that death has lost its sting (1 Corinthians 15:55); no wonder we read that we have no long-term home in this world but are looking forward to the home which is to come (Hebrews 13:14). No wonder Paul wrote that he saw himself as pressing on to the goal (Philippians 3:14).

The more one thinks along these lines, the

more one sees that the human, or 'earthly', viewpoint is diametrically opposed to the Christian viewpoint. In the flesh – that is, before we surrender our lives to the Lord – we are basically the slaves of our past and of our future. What we are is governed by the circumstances of our upbringing, tempered by what we have inherited in our genes from earlier generations. Moreover, before we accept Christ, we have *no* assurance about the future. Having no belief in anyone who is bigger than ourselves, we are basically concerned with our own well-being (even though we may perceive that our well-being is enhanced if we lead an unselfish life, rather than letting ourselves be self-centred).

In contrast, in the Christian approach to life we know that we have a heavenly Father who loves us with a love which is beyond our imagining. We can accept ourselves as we are, without having to put on airs and graces, because He loves us as we are. We can accept that we are imperfect and indeed, by His standards, utterly sinful, for we know that, having handed ourselves over to Him, for Him to do with us just what He wants, we can rely on Him gradually to cleanse us, to change us, and to refine us, until ultimately we shall be perfect, and like Him.

We remember that it was in dying for us on the cross that Jesus broke Satan's hold on us. It was then that He set us free from the bondage to Satan and to self which mankind had chosen at the time of the fall, and has inherited ever since. It was then that, in rising triumphantly the first Easter morning, Jesus conquered death and opened the way for us to enter the glory of eternal life (Romans 5:17).

At Easter, we can once again experience something of the wonder of those early disciples. On the Friday they had been overcome with a shattering sense of despair and disillusionment, when they saw their beloved young leader defeated (as they thought) and killed. Then, as the events of the first Easter day unfolded, they came to realise that Jesus' death had been turned into victory beyond their wildest dreams. As He returned to His Father to reign in glory, they knew He was was to be with them, and with their children's children, for evermore.

Jesus told them, 'Surely I am with you always, to the very end of the age' (Matthew 28:20). Jesus revealed the Father to us and it is to His glory that we look forward, now, ourselves, for eternity.

CHAPTER 27

# The Humility of God

I remember once talking with an elderly lady who was arranging the flowers in church. She had never married and she lived alone. We were talking about our faith. 'The Christian faith,' she assured me, 'is an on-going love affair with Jesus!' From the joy in her face, it was clear that she knew this from her own experience.

Part of loving Him is getting to know Him better and better as a Person. (He is definitely 'personal', even if He is *more* than a person. Certainly He can't be *less* than a person!) If we are asked to describe what we know of the nature of God, our first thought is probably to quote 1 John 4:8: 'God is love'. Clearly His love is fundamental. But we do well to ponder His character further. Recently I find I have been thinking about the sheer humility of God – and humility is not usually the first attribute that comes to mind as we contemplate His glory.

The Jews of old had a strong awareness of the awesome holiness of God. They had a very real glimpse of the majesty and splendour of God, enthroned on high. They realised that His purity was so great that sin simply couldn't exist in His presence. For hundreds of years before Jesus was born, they didn't dare even to say His personal name aloud, for fear of committing blasphemy.

All this is true. But at the same time we need to remember His humility. Paul had His humility in mind when he wrote of Jesus:

> 'Who, being in very nature God,
> did not consider equality with God
> something to be grasped,
> but made himself nothing,
> taking the very nature of a servant,
> being made in human likeness...
> he humbled himself.'
>
> (Philippians 2:6–8)

The other day, as I was praying, the thought came to me that I should, as it were, stand up and look Jesus straight in the eyes, as one man looks at another; but I felt this must be blasphemy! How could I, a mere man, look into the face of Jesus, as I would a man who was my equal? How could I, a sinner, albeit redeemed by Jesus, look Him direct in the eyes? My part surely was to fall down before Him, and beat my breast, saying, 'God, have mercy on me, a sinner' (Luke 18:13)?

Yet while this is indeed true, I believe the other is true, too. I believe the Lord's love for us is so great and so wonderful that He wants to raise us up, so that we may indeed rejoice in this intimate, one-to-one relationship. Jesus expressed His longing for us to be raised up to Him when He said, 'Be perfect therefore, as your heavenly Father is perfect' (Matthew 5:48). Is it not a staggering thought that the Son of the living God actually wants us to become like God? Was there ever such humility? And it is not for us to reject this side of His nature in a kind of false humility. If He loves us as much as this, we must accept it. Paul tells us that we are actually co-heirs with Christ (Romans 8:17).

Again one sees His humility in the words He told John to pass on to the church in Laodicea: 'Here I am! I stand at the door and knock. If anyone hears my voice and opens the door, I will come in' (Revelation 3:20). Can you imagine this humility in an earthly ruler? See how He is content to be ignored, passed by, and overlooked today by the vast majority of mankind!

It is the same with His language given by the Holy Spirit. So many people find it hard to believe that saying a few incomprehensible words can have any effect at all! And yet it is a language of power – powerful to roll back Satan, powerful as we seek to resist temptation, extraordinarily powerful indeed when we may be suffering with pain. It would be easier for us to take this in if we remembered that humility and unobtrusiveness are a part of God's nature.

In some ways it would be so much easier for us mortal men and women to understand if He wasn't so humble! If only He were a bit more flamboyant, we think to ourselves, if only He would show His hand more freely! If only He would be a bit impatient and reveal Himself more obviously!

But as we think these thoughts we realise that they are not of God. As humans we are always compromising, always settling for what is second best. But God is perfect. He always desires what is perfect.

CHAPTER 28

# Listening in Prayer

Jesus saw Himself as our Shepherd and us as His sheep. 'He calls his own sheep by name ... and his sheep follow him because they know his voice' (John 10:3–4). But sometimes it seems that sheep are not good at recognising the voice of their Shepherd. Often people come to us at the Mission who are not clear at all whether the 'voice' they are hearing is from Satan or from Jesus. We all need to recognise the voice of the Good Shepherd and to be clear which voice is which.

(In using the word 'voice' I have in mind the inner thought or prompting of which we can all be aware. It is not unknown for people today to hear the Lord speaking with an audible human voice, but it is not common, and I am not referring to that.)

If we become aware that we are being prompted by a feeling of fear, we need to recognise that that 'voice' is not from the Lord. Fear is Satan's commonest weapon. It is true that, especially in the Old Testament, much is said about fearing God. Fear, in that sense, though, means standing in awe of Him and being aware of His glorious majesty and power. Fear in that sense isn't the destructive force of fear which is what we usually have in mind when we talk about fear.

Perhaps we aren't conscious of fear as we go about our daily lives. But are we always free from anxiety and worry? These are merely different aspects of fear and they get between us and Jesus; they interrupt the power line of love between Him and us, upon which we need to depend. After all, if we are worried or afraid, it shows that we aren't trusting Him. If we are not trusting Him, how can we think of loving Him? And He said that loving Him was the single most important thing in life.

Fear 'grips' us, it causes tension; and tension inhibits many of the natural functions both of our minds and of our bodies. Look how many sicknesses today are induced by stress or tension!

If we are aware of the voice of fear we need to recognise that voice as being of Satan and not of Jesus; and we need to dismiss it from our minds. Those of us who were on active service during World War Two, and many others who have borne the brunt of enemy action, will have felt fear; at those times it was essential not to let the fear deflect us from what we had to do, but to press on, despite the fear.

It is easier to pray for a childlike trust in Jesus than to pray against the worry or the fear. After all, if we trust Him, we can't then be afraid! We can indeed go one step further and make a rule: 'Whenever you hear the lying voice of Satan, think of the opposite and thank Jesus for it.'

By contrast, the 'voice' of the Lord is the 'still small voice' which Elijah heard (1 Kings 19:12,

AV). When we are hearing the Lord aright we are aware of His peace and of His calm certainty. Often we are aware of a little bubbling song of joy in our hearts. When we are weighing up which of two alternative paths the Lord is leading us to follow, do we not come to feel that we have peace as we contemplate one path, and no peace as we think of the other? Almost always the path which gives us peace is where God's voice is leading us.

A voice which Satan often uses is the voice of guilt. In fact I believe that a feeling of guilt is invariably from Satan. I know that if I think back over my life to a specific incident when, many years ago, I clearly and obviously sinned, it wasn't in fact a feeling of guilt which followed, but it was an intense longing to be washed clean and never to touch that thing again. That was the voice of the Lord. I prayed earnestly and I knew then that I had been forgiven.

I believe, however, that when one is feeling guilt, there is a subconscious thought in one's mind: 'Now I've gone and done it; I don't think I could be forgiven for having done this.' But the Lord loves to forgive! We've heard most sins confessed at the Mission, even the deliberate and sustained worship of Satan. But we have no experience of the Lord withholding His forgiveness. Jesus said: 'There will be more rejoicing in heaven over one sinner who repents than over ninety-nine righteous persons' (Luke 15:7).

When we are feeling weighed down by the hopeless feeling of guilt, we need to think of the opposite and to thank Jesus: 'Thank You, Lord, that when I confess my sin You forgive me, and You cleanse me from all unrighteousness' (see

1 John 1:9). Or we can pray more simply: 'Thank You, Jesus, that this feeling of guilt is a lie from Satan and that the truth is that You have cleansed me and that You have set me free.' There is no condemnation for those who are in Christ Jesus (Romans 8:1).

Again, we may hear the voice of Satan lying to us, telling us that we are no good. We can then think of the opposite and thank Jesus: 'Thank You, Jesus, that You accept me just as I am!' If we like, we can add: '... and, if I'm good enough for You to love me, Lord, then I'm good enough for *anyone*!' Never forget, when we hear Satan's voice lying to us, we need to think of the opposite and to thank Jesus for it.

Paul used a different metaphor when he wrote to the church in Corinth. Thinking in terms of a battle, he wrote: 'Take captive every thought' (2 Corinthians 10:5). We are to take a firm hold of every thought that comes to us and examine it. If it is from Satan, we are to send it packing and replace it with a positive thought. 'Test everything,' Paul wrote to the Thessalonians (1 Thessalonians 5:21).

CHAPTER 29

# Persist in Prayer

The other day a man telephoned me from the north of England. We had ministered to him when we were invited to Durham a few months ago, and he was in some distress. 'I don't feel Jesus' presence any more,' he said. 'Everything seems to be going wrong.' Finally he cried: 'What can I do?'

I asked him whether he had read his Bible that morning. 'No,' he replied, 'I just don't feel the desire to read my Bible now.'

'What about your prayer time this morning?' I queried.

'I haven't prayed,' came the reply. 'It doesn't seem real any more.'

I said, 'Supposing I gave up eating for a week. Wouldn't I feel weak and faint?'

'Yes,' he replied.

I told him this was precisely his situation. He had given up on prayer and Bible reading and it was therefore hardly surprising that spiritually he was in a weak state. He mustn't give in. Jesus said, 'Watch and pray so that you will not fall into temptation' (Matthew 26:41).

Some of us become irregular in our daily 'quiet

times' because it has become difficult. Others lead busy lives and have allowed their time with the Lord to become shorter, as it has got crowded out by all the things they tell themselves they have to do. It is so easy to get into the habit of thinking that everything depends on us, and if we don't get through all the jobs which are weighing so heavily on our shoulders, our world is bound to start falling apart!

How little account this attitude takes of the *response* of God to our prayers! As we pray to Him and fill our minds with Him, our burdens fall away, everything begins to come back into focus again, and we experience the wonder of His peace. But if we cut short our time of prayer, we go through the day feeling rushed, we lose things, we forget things, and we finish the day feeling exhausted. How wise was the person who said: 'Everyone needs half an hour alone with the Lord each day – except when they are busy and are really pressed for time. Then the minimum they can get by with is three quarters of an hour.'

If we obey His command and give Him enough time each day, we will retain this inner peace, and everything will go more smoothly. In particular we will find that we actually get through more of our jobs than if we have skimped our time of prayer.

During the 1914–18 war this was found to be equally true of the weekly day of rest. There was a desperate need of ammunition for the gunners on the Western front and certain armaments factories were put on a seven-day week. All the factory workers volunteered to work seven days a week until the crisis was resolved. To begin with, weekly production naturally went up as a result of the extra working day. But in six months, the weekly rate of production was actually lower than when those same factories were working a six-day week. Thus, once again, we see how intensely practical Christianity is, and we recognise the wisdom of God when He decided: 'Six days you shall labour and do all your work but the seventh day ... you shall not do any work' (Exodus 20:9, 10). It is the same God who tells us to 'pray without ceasing' (1 Thessalonians 5:17, AV).

We need our time with the Lord each day. Most people prefer to start the day with this time of prayer and inner strengthening. But if we are more alert in the evenings, that may be the better time for us. But even then we will need to have a certain time of prayer before we set out on the business of the day.

At one of our annual healing conferences at High Leigh, in Hertfordshire, Harry Greenwood was our main speaker and when he arrived we were talking about ministry. 'There will be many people here who are seeking individual ministry,' I said. That he and his wife were ready to minister to people's needs was shown by the way they stayed up till the small hours of the morning, giving of themselves. But he said to me: 'They must nonetheless do their own homework.'

We find there is sometimes a tendency for people to seek ministry first from one person and then from another, as they look for the quick answer to their problems. One of the main points of the Mission here is to minister to such people's needs. But sometimes there comes a moment when one has to say: 'You are trying to find from men what you can only find yourself, direct from God.'

There is a man who telephones us with great regularity for prayer. When I answer the phone I now say to him: 'You pray first and I'll follow.' Jesus never spoon-feeds us. I've come to see that it is right to get that man himself to pray to the Lord, out loud. Then, I'm only too happy to join in with him, committing him to the Lord.

The voice which says: 'You know you can't read your Bible today; you know you are unable to pray properly,' is simply the voice of Satan. As Jesus said, Satan is 'a liar and the father of lies' (John 8:44). We need to resist him resolutely and we then find, once again, the truth of what James wrote: 'Resist the devil, and he will flee from you' (James 4:7).

He does.

In Luke 18:1 we read that Jesus told His disciples a parable 'to show them that they should always pray and not give up'.

CHAPTER 30

# What Actually Happens at Holy Communion

Audrey and I have always gone to church. But for the first fifteen years of our married life we were only, as it were, 'pew-fillers'. We certainly did not know Jesus personally then.

We had it worked out quite carefully. There were three reasons why we chose to go at 8 a.m. First, it was the shortest service, so you got it over quickest, and were then free for the rest of the day. Secondly, you knew that the vicar would be in a hurry for his breakfast, so you avoided being roped in to help with anything in the church. But there was a third reason which in those days we found hard to define. Somehow even then we felt that there was something which mattered in the Communion service.

At the end of the Middle Ages, people were burnt at the stake over the question of whether the bread and wine changed physically into Jesus' body and blood during the prayer of consecration. I don't believe there are many people nowadays who would claim such a physical transformation.

Sadly, I think most people today are quite indifferent to this question – and I think that attitude of indifference is probably more hurtful to Jesus than any other. If I spent time and trouble, and expense too, on buying you a lovely present, I think if I had to choose I would almost sooner have you fling it in my face than see you just put it down and never give it another thought. Indifference can be wounding.

But what does happen when the person at the altar consecrates the bread and the wine? Let us think for a moment of what is meant when we read that our bodies are the temple of the Holy Spirit (1 Corinthians 6:19). If you laid a man down on an operating table and, taking a surgeon's knife, cut him open, you would readily identify the different physical organs in his body. But you would never come upon part of his body to which you could point and say, 'That is the Holy Spirit living in him.' The Holy Spirit living in us has no tangible form. Indeed, if you dissect a human being, and then dissect an animal, the component parts are much the same. You never find the eternal Spirit in tangible form in the human being.

I believe that illustrates how the Spirit of Jesus comes into the bread and the wine during the prayer of consecration. As a priest I have celebrated Communion many, many times and I always believed that the change took place with Jesus' words, 'This is my body', 'This is my blood'. I remember when Audrey and I were ministering to a woman who had very unusual discernment. As I consecrated the elements she said that in her spirit she saw the wine changing with Jesus' words, 'This is my blood of the new covenant.'

I think all of us would accept that in some way there is spiritual strengthening as we share in Holy Communion. Often, however, we see spiritual truths more clearly when we are engaged in the spiritual warfare.

When we are ministering deliverance we always start by having a little service of Communion. On a number of occasions, as we have offered the chalice to the person who is demonised, there has been a pause like the calm before the storm. Then, without warning, there is an outburst of rage and the person will seize the chalice from us and fling it across the room. This wouldn't happen with ordinary, unconsecrated wine.

If the person is demonised, the unclean things in them cannot stand the blood of Jesus. Sometimes the person who is demonised has difficulty taking the bread or the wafer after it has been consecrated. They may try and crumple it in their fingers and drop it on the floor rather than consume it. But for the person with an unclean spirit it is particularly the wine which causes problems. It seems physically to burn them as they swallow it down – something that does not apply if the person is free.

Recently we have been ministering to a woman who has for many years indulged in 'out of the body' experiences which in her case are not under her control. They are extremely painful for her, and they are certainly not of the Lord. We have found that if we anoint her on her forehead with consecrated wine, she comes back immediately. This wouldn't happen with plain wine which had not been consecrated.

Often in one of the more lengthy deliverance

sessions we will give the person the chalice, with the blood of Jesus, every half hour or so. In deliverance one always needs the person's co-operation and we know from experience that as they take the Communion cup again it is like giving them a spiritual shot in the arm.

Of recent years we feel the Lord has been telling us that He wants both those who work at the Healing Mission and the building itself to be absolutely cleansed and pure for Him. In prayer, we 'cover' ourselves with the blood of Jesus every morning as we take Communion, and we cleanse every room periodically 'in the name of Jesus, under the sign of His cross and in the power of His blood', as we sprinkle a few drops of the consecrated wine in the centre of the room. We always cleanse the room immediately someone has left who has been to us for deliverance.

I know in days gone by I would have tended to mock: 'How on earth can there be any spiritual change in a substance just by the speaking of a few words?' In answer, I find myself remembering the first house which we were asked to exorcise. It had poltergeists. They were harmless, but they were frankly a nuisance for the three teenage girls living there. We simply blessed some water from the kitchen tap, speaking the word of God over it, and then again we spoke forth the word of God and commanded the poltergeists to leave the house. It was completely cleared. If one is in the will of God, and speaks forth His word, it does have a spiritual effect.

God said: 'My word that goes out from my mouth ... will not return to me empty, but will accomplish ... the purpose for which I sent it' (Isaiah 55:11).

CHAPTER 31

# God is Supernatural

For many people the word 'supernatural' conjures up a feeling of horror, and often that feeling will be right. Yet there are other times when to think of the supernatural simply in terms of horror misses something fundamental in the Christian faith.

The supernatural is real. I remember many years ago my parents were staying on a farm in South Africa and the farm was suffering badly from a prolonged drought. The farmer (clearly not a Christian!) called in the local witch-doctor and within forty-eight hours there was a torrential downpour over the whole of the farm except for one corner. They called back the witch-doctor to whom they had paid a fee, and asked why there had been no rain in that corner. In reply the witch-doctor said that he had done his magic round the boundary of the whole farm except for that one corner where it hadn't rained.

I remember, also, the occasion many years ago when Audrey and I were in Sri Lanka. I forget whether it was a Buddhist or a Hindu festival but the local holy man was being carried round suspended from a bamboo framework. But instead of being suspended on a swinging chair, he was hanging on meat-hooks threaded through his skin – and there was no bleeding.

I turn, then, to the fascination of the supernatural. I think of Veronica (not her real name) who had held a leading position in a Satanic community for more than thirty years. Some years ago she came to Jesus through our ministry here, and I remember we asked her what the fascination was in her former life. 'Power!' she replied unhesitatingly. She told us that what drew her to Satanism and kept her in it was the power it gave her over other people. (She also told us that eight other people had tried to escape from that Satanic community and every one of them had finished up by committing suicide. She was the ninth – and she was, indeed, an unusually strong character.)

For my next example of the fascination of the supernatural, I turn to a spiritualist séance. I have never been to a séance myself, but I think one can imagine the forbidden thrill of the darkened room, perhaps a mysterious crystal ball on the table, and the upturned glass moving of its own accord answering questions which were being put to the so-called spirits of the dead.

Those who have lost a loved one are sometimes beguiled into attending a spiritist session in their longing to be in touch once more with the one who has 'passed on'. But we are clearly warned against this in Deuteronomy 18:11–12. There is nothing biblical about such practices and whatever comfort seems to be given is not, I believe, from God – and therefore can only be satanic.

I think the fascination of the supernatural –

that is, the satanic supernatural – is that it holds out the beguiling thought of enabling human beings to be like God, with knowledge of the future, and power over other people which mankind is not meant to have. It is worth remembering the sin committed by mankind in the Garden of Eden: Adam and Eve believed a lie. The lie lay in denying the existence of God, or in relegating God, the Creator of the universe, to irrelevance.

> 'The lie purports man to be God, having the right to do his own will and to seek his own desires. It presumes that all that God is, and all that God has said and made, is inferior or inadequate and that man can remedy or improve the deficiency. Viewing God, or treating God, in this way is our greatest sin and causes our basic problem.' (With acknowledgement to Harnhill newsletter.)

Everything I have quoted about the supernatural so far has been of the satanic side. Everything I have quoted touches on forbidden activities for the Christian, and it is very right that we should shrink from all such activities. But the supernatural is not merely the realm of Satan. How important it is that we should not let the baby out with the bath-water! The fundamental truth which we need to remember is that God Himself is supernatural.

There are so many churches up and down the country where the congregation wants a nice 'safe' Christianity where the supernatural is firmly barred and where everything can be safely predicted. The power of the living God to heal and to make whole, and to guide His people, will be denied in these churches and, in time, they will come to die on their feet. Christianity which denies the supernatural nature of God is a dead religion.

Jesus said to the woman at the well: 'God is spirit, and his worshippers must worship in spirit and in truth' (John 4:24). If God is 'spirit' then it must follow that God is supernatural. It is also helpful to understand that here, as so often in St John's Gospel, the word 'truth' is interchangeable with the word 'reality'.

Jesus was saying that God is supernatural and He is real.

Many years ago, before Jackie Pullinger became well-known, I invited some two hundred people to a meeting in our village school to hear this girl from Hong Kong. As she began to speak my first reaction was of horror. 'I find religion so boring!' she declared. The thought raced through my mind: Why ever have I gathered two hundred people to hear a Christian speaker who starts by denigrating her religion?

But I needn't have worried. 'Yes,' Jackie said, 'I find religion boring and dull, but I just love Jesus!' A Jesus one can relate to, and look to for guidance and help, is quite simply supernatural.

Someone has said that as Christians we need to be 'naturally supernatural'. We are spiritual animals and will never find peace until we find that our spiritual needs are met by a supernatural God.

CHAPTER 32

# The Exercise of Self-Discipline

There are times when I almost feel sorry for the Pharisees of Jesus' day! He never minced his words, did he? Similarly, the rich young ruler didn't exactly like it when Jesus told him to sell off all his possessions.

We sometimes find ourselves speaking firmly to someone who has come to see us; we find ourselves saying things which may be for his good but which, nonetheless, he would rather not hear!

Take the need for self-discipline. After all, who likes self-discipline? Wouldn't we all prefer to be without it? Yet it is often what we need. And God disciplines us! This comes through so clearly in Hebrews 12:5–12, especially when the writer says, 'God disciplines us for our good.' I remember when I was still a schoolboy my house-master said to me: 'Andy, surely you can see that boys are happier when they have some discipline?' I had to admit he was right. It's true of girls, too, and of grown-ups.

I believe the need for us to exercise self-discipline is greater today than it ever has been before.

In days gone by, if you wanted to go somewhere and you weren't rich enough to own a horse, you had no choice but to walk. It was no use feeling tired! Either you went on walking, regardless of whether you were tired or not – or else you didn't get to your destination. Similarly many of us forget that up to 1914 the commonest form of employment for men in this country was working on the land. There was far less farm machinery then. Hard physical work was involved. One just couldn't get by without disciplining oneself. Paul had this in mind when he wrote, 'If a man will not work, he shall not eat' (2 Thessalonians 3:10).

I remember Nellie, the waitress who often served my lunch when I started working in the City. She used to recall that she had brought up five children in the 1930s. 'They all grew up fit and strong – and they're all happily married now!' she would add with a real sense of achievement in her voice. But like many working-class families before the war, they had very little money; things were hard for them and she didn't succeed in bringing up her family without exercising constant self-discipline.

However, for many of us today the business of living is much easier. Everything is 'instant-this' and 'labour-saving-that'. Many people are able to get through life without ever really exerting themselves. They may well experience tension and strain; they may well not be particularly happy; but they can get through without exercising much discipline. If they want to go somewhere they use public transport, and most of the physical effort has been taken out of work.

I think of Mary (not her real name) who came

to see me. She said she often didn't get up until the middle of the afternoon. 'What is there to get up for?' she asked. Her husband had died young, her children were in care and she was living on social security. What indeed was there to get up for? Yet, as I compared her with Nellie, there was no doubt which was the happier woman!

There was no plan in Mary's life, and there was no structure in her day; there was no self-discipline. She told me that the three props in her day-to-day life were alcohol, cigarettes and the drugs the doctors prescribed for her. She agreed with me that her only hope was Jesus. 'I want to kick all my three props and only rely on Him,' she said. The question was how to help her to do this. There are not many people who are spiritually strong enough to spend all day in solitary prayer. I couldn't. Nor could she. But she accepted that by exercising some degree of self-discipline she could draw closer to Jesus and she would herself grow in spiritual strength. She would be happier too.

We started by agreeing the time she should get up in the morning. We planned what time she should start her quiet time and, almost as important, we planned what time she should end it. If we are unemployed it is so easy to keep putting off our time of prayer right through the day, until eventually we are too sleepy for any worthwhile prayer. But also we need to be disciplined in having a fixed time to end it; otherwise we will go dreaming on for hours, again without actually getting down to real prayer.

I asked if she ever took any exercise. 'Not if I can help it!' was the answer. There is much sense in the motto of the Army Physical Training Corps, 'Mens sana in corpore sano' – a healthy mind and a healthy body do indeed go together. We will not be healthy without regular fresh air and exercise. We agreed when Mary was to go for a walk each day and when she would return.

Then there is the question of food. A few years ago before our daughter Caroline became a Christian and when she was still practising acupuncture, a boy of nineteen came to her for help. I forget what his trouble was, but she started questioning him about his life-style. It emerged that he was existing to a large extent on a diet of potato crisps and ginger pop. Caroline saw that so long as this continued it was no use her trying to help him. She told him to discipline himself to eat a sensible balanced diet; then she would help him. Countless people, especially those who live alone, don't bother to eat properly. We need to discipline ourselves in what we eat as well as in how much – neither too much nor too little.

In the same way, we see the need for self-discipline when people come to us suffering from depression. Depression sets in when there is an emptiness in our hearts. If we can help someone to fill that emptiness by continually thanking Jesus for what he or she has got – and going on from there to praise Him – the depression will gradually lose its hold and then finally go. The depressive needs to discipline himself to turn outwards, away from himself and towards Jesus.

These are some of the ways in which self-discipline leads to greater 'wholeness', that is, greater healing and well-being of our body, mind, soul and spirit. 'Wholeness' is what the Lord is longing to give us; 'wholeness' is one of the meanings of the Greek word for salvation. The Greek word *sozo*, which means 'to save', 'rescue', also means 'to restore to health', 'to heal'. The Lord wants to help us in every area of our lives!

But what of the person who finds self-discipline difficult? Indeed, what of the person who gets depressed because he is always trying to discipline himself and seems never to succeed? Perhaps it would help to fast. One of the advantages of fasting is the self-discipline which is involved. There is a mild discomfort even in fasting for twenty-four hours and that discomfort needs to be overcome.

I believe when we fast it shows three people that we mean business in our spiritual lives. It shows Satan we mean business (he doesn't like it!); it shows Jesus we mean business, and that brings joy to His heart; and perhaps most important is the fact that, when we fast, we show ourselves that in our spiritual lives we mean business.

CHAPTER 33

# Letting Go of Anger

Is it right to be angry? Or is it wrong? Many people are puzzled about anger.

Psychiatrists voice the conventional wisdom of today. They warn of the dangers of bottling up anger: 'You must let your anger out!' they tell us. This is right. If we repress our anger and don't let it out, the anger isn't dealt with; it remains there festering deep within us.

But how are we to deal with it? If we go round venting our anger on other people, we hurt them; that cannot be within the will of a God of love. Indeed there is a subtle and refined form of selfishness which says: 'I've got to get rid of my anger and I don't care what effect it has on the person on whom I take it out!'

The other day we had someone at the Mission who had been emotionally shattered by a Christian friend. 'You are not in the Lord's will,' she had shouted at her. 'You're not looking after your mother,' she accused her. 'And where is your duty to your husband?' she added. Subsequently the friend had admitted: 'I was just getting rid of my anger.' The person who came to us had in no way been the cause of the anger!

Many people will point to the example of Jesus. 'Jesus was angry,' they will tell you. They point to the time when Jesus cleansed the Temple, casting out all those who were buying and selling goods and exchanging money. Often, however, they forget that this was no sudden outburst of rage on Jesus' part. We read in Mark 11 that Jesus went to the Temple in the evening, after His triumphal entry into Jerusalem, and He had a good look round. But since it was already late He then went out to Bethany. It was the following day that He entered the Temple area and began driving out those who were buying and selling there. It is clear from the full account that Jesus looked round calmly at what He saw, and then went away and slept on it and, no doubt, prayed deeply through the situation. Then He went deliberately to the Temple to carry out what He saw needed to be done. Although the cleansing of the Temple is recorded in each of the four Gospels, it is interesting that in none of the records are we actually told that Jesus was angry.

In the Sermon on the Mount Jesus quoted the old commandment from Exodus 20: 'Do not murder,' and then went on: 'But I tell you that anyone who is angry with his brother will be subject to judgment' (Matthew 5:22). James writes: 'Everyone should be quick to listen, slow to speak and slow to become angry' (James 1:19), whilst we read in Psalm 37:8, 'Refrain from anger and turn from wrath.' Paul wrote: 'In your anger do not sin' (Ephesians 4:26), but he was quoting from Psalm 4:4, where the full passage reads: 'In your anger do not sin; when you are on your beds, search your hearts and be silent.'

Sometimes when I am praying with someone who is beset by some physical affliction I find the anger rising in me. Am I angry with that person? Of course I am not. It is anger with Satan which I feel rising within me – anger that Satan should have dared to afflict a lovely Christian person with this particular sickness or infirmity. The only time we are told in the Gospel stories that Jesus was angry was when He healed the man with the shrivelled hand in the synagogue. We read: 'He looked round at them in anger and, deeply distressed at their stubborn hearts, said to the man, "Stretch out your hand"' (Mark 3:5). We remember that Jesus, though always loving the sinner, hates the sin. Anger with Satan or with sin seems acceptable for the Christian.

But there are times when we are angry and it is not with Satan that we are angry. Anger can bubble up to the surface of our mind with a seemingly irresistible force. We then have to make the decision whether we are going to explode into negative action, or turn to the Lord, perhaps screaming to Him in our pain, but in our screams seeking His appropriate action.

God can then lead us into the action we should take to enable the fire of the anger to be converted into a positive force for good. In that way none of the emotion is suppressed and we feel satisfied. Perhaps someone tells us that we can't do something. As we pray about this our anger turns into a determination that, whatever anyone says, we are actually going to do what we've been told is beyond us!

There are other times when we simply have to recognise that to give way to the anger would be wrong. A man came to us whose wife was having no option but to give up most of each weekend to the task of looking after her sick and elderly mother. As a result his own weekends were being ruined. He was tempted to be angry with either his mother-in-law or his wife. Yet he realised that his mother-in-law couldn't help the fact that she was elderly and sick, whilst he had to admit that his wife was being a really loving daughter in the way she was looking after her own mother. For him to have given way to anger with either of them would simply have been wrong.

In fact that man found the solution when he turned to the Lord and prayed through the situation with Him. Often we are angry because we've been hurt. We need to come to Him in prayer and open our hearts to Him. Then, as we pray through the hurt and as we come closer to the Lord in our relationship of love with Him, we will be able to let the hurt go to Him. That seems to me a sure way of dealing with anger. As we work at it and persist in seeking to draw closer and closer to Him in love, His peace will gently flow into our hearts and, as we receive His peace, first the hurt and then the anger will be gently melted away. That way we are not repressing the anger. We are simply letting it go to Him.

Often as we have prayed through such a situation with someone they have turned to us afterwards and said: 'As you were praying I actually felt something leave me.'

It is wrong for us to bottle up anger and repress it. However, it is equally wrong for us to take out our anger on some other person. We need to take it to the Lord in prayer and let Him deal with it.

CHAPTER 34

# Delayed Healings

Almost all our team shared in the ministry at a recent healing conference where the main speaker was Francis MacNutt. Francis must be one of the more notable people in the healing ministry in America today, and he must have prayed for thousands of people.

One of his main themes was that he sees a definite relationship between the amount of time and effort we invest in prayer, and the amount of healing which we thereby draw down from Jesus. For instance, he said that out of every twenty-five people who are aware of answered prayer for healing, perhaps only one will have received an instantaneous healing. In all the other twenty-four cases, it will be the beginning of a gradual healing or, indeed, of a delayed healing. He went on to say that if they pray for people for a couple of hours a far higher proportion are healed than if they just pray briefly. Very often when they cease praying the healing stops, and he added that this was the experience of everyone he knew in the healing ministry. Our own experience is the same.

Often I feel like crying out: 'Lord, why aren't

You releasing more actual miracles when we pray?' I have come to see that very often the answer is: 'Because I love them too much.' His way is always the perfect way.

That the Lord longs to comfort each of us, His children, to set us free, to heal us and to make us whole and perfect is, to my mind, beyond doubt. But if the Lord always answered prayer for healing with a miracle, there would be no stimulus for us to reach out to Him, to draw closer and closer to Him in prayer.

If I receive partial healing, or if I'm healed and then I lose my healing, I am encouraged to even greater efforts in prayer. 'He must want to heal me,' I say to myself, 'otherwise why should He have bothered to release the degree of healing which He did?' God is not, after all, an inhuman ogre who plays with His children. He is a God of perfect love. Therefore, having started the healing, He must want to complete it and my reaction is to reach out all the more. Thus we draw ever closer to Him in that relationship of love which is the heart of the Christian faith.

I've noticed in our ministry here that when people are healed miraculously, almost always they are left with some other affliction, for the healing of which they just have to battle away in prayer. They will be encouraged in their faith by the miracle. But there will still be the stimulus to move on and draw closer to Jesus in prayer.

Jesus told the story of the widow and the unjust judge to illustrate the need for persistence in prayer. The judge at first refused to give the widow her rights. Then he became exasperated with her constant pleading. '"Even though I don't fear God or care about men," he cried, "yet because this widow keeps bothering me, I will see that she gets justice"' (Luke 18:4–5).

There is a clear biblical example of persistence in prayer in the case of the Syro-Phoenician woman and her daughter (Matthew 15). As we read the account carefully we realise that, to begin with, she pesters Jesus' disciples to set her daughter free. (Her daughter is at home and suffering from some demonic affliction.)

Clearly the disciples either can't or won't help her. Then she comes to Jesus, and to our amazement we find that Jesus completely ignores her. At first sight that seems callous rejection on Jesus' part, but we must wait for the unfolding of the story.

The disciples intervene and ask Jesus to send her away. He doesn't send her away, but He appears to be saying very clearly that He is not going to heal her daughter. One can well imagine the temptation for the woman to give up. Jesus seemingly had made it obvious that He didn't care about her daughter. How many of us today, when our prayer is not answered at once, give up and say: 'Well, I know God heals some people, but He's made it obvious that He's not interested in healing me.'

But the woman is not going to be put off – she actually argues with Jesus. He tells her that it isn't right to take the children's bread and throw it to the dogs. We all remember her retort: 'But even the dogs eat the crumbs that fall from their masters' table.'

Then we have Jesus' lovely reply: He commends

her faith and her daughter is made well from that very hour.

I believe Jesus sensed that the woman had enough faith to hold on. I am quite sure that all the time He was longing to heal her daughter. But He also wanted to test her faith – and let us remember that it is only as our faith is tested that it grows stronger. He gave her the opportunity to hold fast in faith and to reach out to Him. Thus, when He healed her daughter, He had also enabled the mother to grow stronger in faith than before.

When we have prayed for someone's healing we almost always urge them to keep on thanking the Lord that His healing is on the way. This takes faith, particularly if, so far, there is no visible sign of the healing taking place. We may encourage the person by asking: 'Do you believe Jesus was listening when we were praying?' We may continue: 'Do you believe our prayer was in line with the will of a God of perfect love?' If the person accepts that the answer to both questions is 'Yes', then they can thank Him that the answer is on the way. John tells us that whatever we ask in line with His will He hears us and, if we really believe that He has heard us, we have what we have asked for (1 John 5:14–15).

Suppose a friend of mine rings up from Australia. 'I've just been out this morning, Andy,' he says, 'and I've bought you a lovely present. After lunch today I'm going to mail it to you.' Do I say 'thank you' there and then? Yes, of course I do – even before I've received the present. I may be so overcome by my friend's generosity that I actually sit down the following day and write him a letter of thanks – and still before I've received his present.

If we've asked the Lord for something which is in line with His will, then we can confidently thank Him that, it is, as it were, in the mail to us from heaven. We can thank Him confidently, though we have yet to receive it.

It is, I believe, in those repeated little prayers of thanks that we actually draw down more and more of His power to heal. The more time we invest in prayer, the more of His healing we do, in fact, draw down. To put it in different words, it is as we thank Him that we set the seal on our original prayer to Him.

CHAPTER 35

# Sins in Thought

Many of us are familiar with the words of the confession, in which we ask the Lord to forgive us our sins 'in thought, word and deed'.

If we yield to temptation in a shop and, when we think nobody is looking, pop something in our pockets without paying for it, that is clearly a case of sinning 'in deed'. If the shop assistant then runs down the street after us and challenges us with having stolen it, and we turn around, look him straight in the eye, and say, 'I've not taken anything,' that is a sin 'in word'. We would all agree that sins in deed and word are wrong and destructive. But I suspect that many people feel that sins 'in thought' are less serious, since they appear to hurt nobody.

Such a view is mistaken. Sins of wrong thinking are just as deadly as other types of sin. They can harm other people and they most certainly harm the person doing the thinking.

Some years ago our niece was staying with a Christian family. One day she had been criticising the wife, in her mind. She hadn't said anything, but all through the day she had been thinking to herself, 'Why does she do this, this way? I would do it the other way. Why does she have to do it at all?'

Towards evening the other woman turned to our niece. 'I've had a migraine coming on all day,' she said. 'Will you pray for me?'

Our niece reflected, and it struck her that there was a connection between her negative thinking about her hostess and her hostess's migraine.

'I am terribly sorry,' she said. 'I've been thinking negatively about you all day, and I believe it is my thoughts that have brought on the migraine. Will you forgive me?' Her hostess forgave her, the two united again, and the migraine went.

There are many examples of the way we hurt ourselves by our wrong thinking. It is a fact of life that other people tend to take us at our own estimate of ourselves. If we go through life believing that we are not much good at anything then we will find that those around us form the same opinion about us – not very flattering and also not very helpful.

So often if we are afraid of something happening, it is almost as if we were willing it to happen, and it is curious that it then quite often does happen. This happened to Job. He said, 'What I feared has come upon me' (Job 3:25).

I think faith is like a car. It is designed to move forwards but if you particularly want it to go backwards you can put it into reverse gear. Faith is meant to encourage us to believe that what is good is going to come about. But I believe there is such a thing as negative faith. When we allow our minds to become so dominated by something negative or harmful which we are afraid is going to happen to us, somehow it is as if we are actually having faith for that dire thing to happen.

I remember the head of one of London's famous teaching hospitals saying to Audrey in the days before they invented the modern therapies for the cure of cancer, 'We normally don't tell patients when they have cancer because the physical spread of the cancer will actually be accelerated if the person is afraid, either of their suffering or ultimately of dying.' What we think can influence our bodily functions.

Again, there is a connection between our thought patterns and the functioning of our immune system. Those who let themselves become a prey to worrying will not have 'the peace of God which passes understanding' but instead will suffer from tension. It is a medical fact that undue tension in the mind can have an adverse effect on the working of the immune system.

If however we turn ourselves and put our complete trust in Jesus we shall receive His peace, and we see so often here in the Mission that there is much healing if a person can receive the peace of God.

How then are we to control our thought patterns? Is the human brain so constructed that we can control with our wills what our minds are thinking? The answer is that we are unable to stop ourselves thinking along a particular line of thought unless we do something else as well. The more we say to ourselves, 'I'm *not* going to think about that,' the more we find ourselves thinking about it!

However, if we find ourselves thinking negatively we are able to direct our thoughts to what is positive. If we fill our minds with positive thinking we will find that the negative thinking has, as it were, become squeezed out of our minds. Paul understood about the necessity of directing our thoughts in the right and constructive direction. He proclaims: 'Take captive every thought' (2 Corinthians 10:5). 'Whatever is true, whatever is noble, whatever is right, whatever is pure, whatever is lovely ... think about such things' (Philippians 4:8).

Whenever we catch ourselves thinking a negative thought we need to train ourselves to switch over to thinking about the opposite and positive thought. The negative thought will have been from Satan whose very nature is to torment and to destroy. It follows therefore that the opposite line of thought will be from God who is perfect love and who by His very nature is always seeking to heal and to make perfect.

CHAPTER 36

# The Sovereignty of God

Let us look at two accounts of Jesus healing blind men. In John 9 we read that Jesus spat on the ground, made some mud with the saliva, and put it on the man's eyes. He told him to go and wash in the pool of Siloam; and the man who had been blind 'came home seeing'. Then in Mark 10 Jesus merely spoke to the blind man, and he was healed.

Perhaps the two men met a while later. They would soon have been talking excitedly about what had been for each of them the most wonderful day in his life – the day when all at once he was able to see perfectly. One can imagine each recounting how Jesus had healed him, one with a paste made by Jesus with dust and His saliva, the other simply by Jesus' words. When they turned, each to go to his own home, one can imagine the first man muttering to himself, 'Poor fellow, he thinks Jesus healed him. But Jesus didn't use His saliva on his eyes; He can't have healed him properly!'

Jesus loves each of us as an individual, each with a love that is unique to us. It is so easy to think that because Jesus has healed one person one way, then it must follow that He will heal the next person the same way. God is sovereign and is not to be pushed about by mere mortals like us.

We see the same pattern of the Lord healing in different ways. I think of Cedric, in his early fifties, who had been a depressive for many years. He was healed in ten minutes flat at the altar rail at one of our first Healing Services. I think then of Eileen, who was also healed of depression, around the same time, but in her case she had to come for four or five appointments spread over seven months or so. It is no use our saying, 'Why didn't He heal each of them instantaneously?' God is sovereign.

Is it a mere theological nicety to recognise that God is sovereign? After all, 'sovereign' is not a word in everyday use. We don't talk to our neighbour on the bus about so-and-so being 'sovereign'.

Many people, perhaps under the influence of New Age thinking, are ready to accept that there is some kind of benign force or power in the universe without being ready to accept that that force is a personal God. God may be much more than a person but He certainly is not less, and since I know of no word which really conveys the meaning of a God who is more than a person I can only think of God as being 'a person'. But if God were less than a person, if He were after all only some benign force, then He could not love. Yet love is the creative and dynamic power which flows from a God of perfect love. If we think of God as a being who is less than a person, we are thinking of a God who cannot love; Satan is very happy indeed if that should be our mistaken concept of God!

But God's personality is not limited as ours is. He is much bigger, He is much greater. The only word I know which gives expression to that is when we describe God as 'sovereign'. God is complete in Himself, He is free and independent, and although we have His Spirit dwelling within us He is at the same time out there over against us, perfect, complete and sovereign.

Let us go back to the Bible and look at how God responded to prayer in three separate, but similar, instances. The early Christians met much opposition and they were often thrown into prison. We read in Acts 5 that when Peter and some of the apostles were arrested and put in the public jail, an angel of the Lord opened the doors of the jail and brought them out. Yet, when enquiry was made the following morning, the jail was found still securely locked, with the guards standing at the doors. Clearly the prayers of the early church for the release of the apostles were answered by God and, on this occasion, he released the apostles through a miracle – he sent an angel who opened locked doors and then closed them again.

We then turn to Acts 16. Paul and Silas were in prison and characteristically were spending the night praying and singing hymns to God! 'Suddenly there was such a violent earthquake that the foundations of the prison were shaken', and the prison doors flew open. Prisons in those days were not large concrete blocks and it is quite understandable that the result of an earthquake would be to loosen the doorposts of each entrance and that consequently the doors would have swung open on their hinges.

Again God answered prayer for the release of the two Christian leaders but this time he worked through a natural event, the earthquake and its consequences.

For my third example, I refer to Paul's last imprisonment. There was no answer by God to the prayers which must have been sent up for his release. Paul was not released. It is no use our questioning God and asking why He chose to react to prayer in different ways on those three occasions. God is sovereign and He is not to be boxed in by any human rules.

Again, we can take examples from today. Jennifer Rees-Larcombe had been in a wheelchair for eight years, Julie Sheldon was in hospital with dystonia, with no prospect of ever leaving, whilst Jenny Richards, with motor neurone disease, was unable to speak, or even to eat normally. Jennifer was healed instantaneously; Julie was healed miraculously, too, but it took several months; Jenny lived a year longer than the doctors thought possible, and was thus able to see her very remarkable testimony, *Love Never Ends*, published before she died.

It is true that we need to know about the nature of God. As we often say here, you need to know the kind of God you are dealing with. We need to take in, beyond any shadow of doubt, that God is perfect love, always and without any exception. We need to know that it is always the will of a God of perfect love to comfort His people, to set them free, to build them up – and eventually to heal, to make whole and to make perfect.

It is necessary for us to be clear in our hearts about the nature and, indeed, the character of

God. Unless we know the kind of God we are dealing with, we shall be unable to trust Him. Unless we are able to put our complete trust in Him I don't believe we are able to surrender ourselves completely to Him in love.

Yet at the same time we must never make the mistake of thinking that because God is perfect love He has *got* to answer our prayer for this or that. We must always remember that God is complete in Himself, He cannot be pushed around by mere mortals. God is, indeed, sovereign. For me the sovereign majesty of God is so well expressed in the closing chapters of the book of Job. Job has been questioning for so long but at last his questions run out and God speaks out of the storm:

> 'Who is this that darkens my counsel
> with words without knowledge?...
> Where were you when I laid the earth's
> foundation?
> Tell me, if you understand....
> Who shut up the sea behind doors
> when it burst forth from the womb,
> when I made the clouds its garment
> and wrapped it in thick darkness...?
> Have you ever given orders to the
> morning,
> or shown the dawn its place...?
> What is the way to the abode of light?
> And where does darkness reside?
> Can you take them to their places?
> Do you know the paths to their
> dwellings?' (Job 38:2–20)

Small wonder that Job was humble when he replied:

'I know that you can do all things;
 no plan of yours can be thwarted....
Surely I spoke of things I did not
 understand,
 things too wonderful for me to know....
My ears had heard of you,
 but now my eyes have seen you.'
(Job 42:2–5)

We will never 'see' the true nature of God unless we perceive that, among all His other attributes, God is, indeed, sovereign.

CHAPTER 37

# Do I Have to Forgive?

Recently three ladies came to the Mission together, each of them suffering with arthritis or rheumatism. As we talked with them, it came out that each of them had been hurt by another person.

'Have you forgiven that person?' we asked.

'No!' came back the reply. 'We don't have to – Jesus says we only have to forgive when the other person apologises first.'

They referred us to Luke 17:3 where Jesus says, 'If your brother sins, rebuke him, *and if he repents, forgive him*' (my italics). Did Jesus really teach that we were to forgive unconditionally, or is our forgiveness to be conditional on the other person first saying sorry?

There are many verses in the Bible which point to the need for us to forgive unconditionally. To take only three of them:

> Jesus said: 'When you stand praying, if you hold anything against anyone, forgive him' (Mark 11:25).

> Paul wrote: 'Be kind and compassionate to one another, forgiving each other' (Ephesians 4:32).

> He also wrote: 'Bear with each other and forgive whatever grievances you may have against one another' (Colossians 3:13).

I believe the Lord always wants us to forgive. If we allow any resentment or bitterness to remain in us, it works like a spiritual cancer. We get screwed up spiritually as a result. We may then get screwed up mentally and in time there may be physical consequences. Quite often an onset of arthritis or rheumatism is preceded by a feeling of resentment or bitterness towards someone.

Often a feeling of resentment is very understandable! We have had people coming here driven almost desperate by lack of sleep as they have lain awake through the night unable to shut out the blaring row of a neighbour's radio. Under those circumstances, I can well imagine myself seething with fury and anger as I tossed and turned, longing to be allowed to go to sleep!

But it isn't right. We need to let go of the anger and the resentment and, once again, receive the peace of God which is beyond all human understanding. We need resolutely to switch our thoughts to Jesus. We need to seek Him to the exclusion of the resentment. We need to allow Him to give us, once more, His wonderful peace – and as we thus enter again into the harmony of love with Him, we find we are able to hand over the anger and bitterness to Him. Often, when one of us has helped someone to pray like that, we have afterwards received the comment, 'I actually felt something go from me.'

Winston Churchill once wrote that it is impossible for the human mind to shut off a particular area of mental activity unless it is consciously replaced with another area of thought. He found that when he went on holiday he couldn't leave behind the problems and the responsibilities of his office unless he deliberately concentrated on something else – hence his taking up painting as a pastime. If, for our part, we want to be free from resentment and bitterness, we need to turn to Jesus and fill our whole mind and heart with His light and His love.

But what, then, of the occasion when Jesus instructed His disciples, '*If your brother repents,* forgive him'? I believe much turns on the meaning of the word 'forgive'. In its fullest sense forgiveness means the restoration of a relationship of love between two people. I can get rid of the resentment in my heart, unilaterally, without the co-operation of the person who originally hurt me, but there cannot be a restoration of a fellowship of love between me and that person unless he, for his part, accepts my forgiveness, and that he can only do if he first admits to being in the wrong. It is impossible, therefore, for there to be forgiveness in the sense of restoring a relationship of love unless the other person plays his part, too. The restoration of that fellowship cannot be achieved by one person only.

Let us look then at how forgiveness works in the relationship between ourselves and the Lord. We have seen that between two human beings the first step is for us to let go of the resentment and allow ourselves to be cleansed from any feelings of anger or bitterness. Clearly, God doesn't have to wrestle with that sort of problem. He is perfect in every way.

But precisely because God is perfect, He's longing all the more for a full restoration of the fellowship of love between Himself and His people. This can only come about when we first turn to Him and tell Him we're sorry for all that we've done wrong. The theme of repentance being followed by the Lord's forgiveness comes often in the Bible. To take another three examples:

> Jesus 'went into all the country around the Jordan, preaching a baptism of repentance for the forgiveness of sins' (Luke 3:3).

> 'Repentance and forgiveness of sins will be preached in his name to all nations, beginning at Jerusalem' (Luke 24:47).

> 'Peter replied, "Repent and be baptised every one of you ... for the forgiveness of your sins"' (Acts 2:38).

This leads to the very practical question, 'How do we repent?' There will be occasions in our lives when, as we lose ourselves in love and adoration of the Lord, we realise quietly that this or that aspect of our lives is, frankly, rather shabby and that we long for Him to set us free from it. It is easy then to say: 'Lord, I am so sorry, I hadn't realised that that was wrong, please cleanse me and wash it away.'

But what of the occasion when we are not aware that there is something in us which needs to be forgiven? Nothing is gained by trying to 'manufacture' sins in order to repent of them, and I'm not too sure of the advantage of some of these printed lists of sins which, it is sometimes suggested, we should read through every week before going to Holy Communion to make sure we have repented of everything we might have done wrong.

I think we need to turn back to Jesus' words: 'Be perfect, therefore, as your heavenly Father is perfect' (Matthew 5:48).

Once we allow our minds to dwell on the utter holiness of the Lord, on His perfect purity and sinlessness, we become aware of how second-rate and shabby we are by comparison. Then it is easy to pray: 'Lord, forgive me for everything which I am, which is not perfect' – and if you're anything like me, that means just about everything! After all, in His love for us, He longs to be allowed to transform us into His own nature so that we may be perfect like Him, and it is as we face up to all that He needs to do in us that we are able, truly, to turn to Him and repent.

The forgiveness follows. We know that the Lord is always longing to forgive us. 'If we confess our sins, he is faithful and just and will forgive us our sins and purify us from all unrighteousness' (1 John 1:9). Once we have repented before the Lord and received His forgiveness, then there is the restoration of that relationship of love which the Lord is always longing to have between Himself and each of His people.

CHAPTER 38

# What Really Happened on Calvary?

Try and call to mind a picture you have seen of Jesus hanging on the cross. Most of us have seen many pictures of the crucifixion and probably the picture in your mind will be a composite, formed from many pictures. But I think all of us can recall some picture of Jesus on the cross.

I suggest that the picture you have in your mind is inaccurate in three ways. Firstly, Jesus will be respectfully clad with a loin-cloth fastened round His waist and reaching well down His thighs. This is one example of the way mankind has recoiled from the sheer horror of what they did to Jesus, for the victim of a Roman crucifixion was always pinned up, stark naked, on the cross. Indeed, we read in the Gospel accounts how the Roman soldiers divided Jesus' clothing among them.

Any picture I have seen of the crucifixion is inaccurate in another respect also. The pictures I call to mind all show a beautifully carpentered cross, balanced in its proportions and with all roughness planed away. As often as not the wood of the cross is polished as well. Furthermore the pictures I have seen have almost invariably shown Jesus raised up on a high cross and well above the heads of the bystanders.

Again, this is religious sentimentality. To the Romans, Jesus was just a common criminal. Why should they have bothered with the appearance of the cross? All they cared about was that it should be strong enough to take the nails and bear the weight of His body.

Furthermore, there would be no sense in having a high cross. That would have been a waste of good timber. It would also have spoiled part of the sport for the crowd. In the Middle Ages our ancestors were accustomed to torment a criminal who was locked in the stocks for a day on the village green. And 2000 years ago there would have been those among the on-lookers who would have exulted in adding to the torment of the victim if his naked body was in their reach.

But any picture I have seen of the crucifixion is inaccurate in a third and more important respect. The pictures I have seen have always concentrated on portraying a man suffering extreme agony. Yet if we had been looking on I believe our attention would have been riveted, not so much by the agony Jesus was undergoing, but by something else.

Don't let us underestimate either the physical or spiritual agony which Jesus underwent. The previous night He had endured a Roman flogging and grown men often died or went mad under the torture of a Roman flogging. The Greeks called it 'opening up' a man's back. The skin was literally torn off Him, leaving His back from His neck to

His knees a mass of twitching, bleeding, human flesh.

Then there would have been the agony of the nails being driven through His hands and His feet, the appalling cramp as the weight of the body was taken on the nails, and in addition to everything else, the dozens of black flies crawling over His wounds, His eyes and His mouth, while Jesus, pinned to the cross, was unable to brush them off.

No. The physical agony was real enough. And while we can only guess at the spiritual agony, as Jesus bore our sins on His own shoulders, and thus was cut off for the only time in His life from His Father in heaven, we can assume that it was even worse than the physical torment.

Had we been watching the crucifixion there would without doubt have been moments when our hearts would have gone out to Jesus and we would have felt unspeakable horror at what he was suffering.

But I believe the dominant thought in our minds would have been one of sheer wonder and amazement. The words on our lips would have been: *'However is He managing to do it?'*

I believe that Jesus was totally in control of the situation the whole time He was on the cross. Years ago we took our children to the Passion Play at Oberammergau. I counted nearly 500 people on the stage during the crucifixion scene. But through it all, the producer had contrived to convey that Jesus was totally in control of what was happening.

Let me give an example. Remember how Jesus called out from the cross in a calm, clear voice asking John to look after His mother, and telling His mother that she would be all right with John to care for her? Only a man who was totally in control of the situation would have been thinking of other people while He was undergoing crucifixion.

What was it that gave Jesus the strength to triumph over the agony? There is a hint of the answer in Hebrews, when the writer refers to Jesus 'who for the joy set before him endured the cross, scorning its shame' (Hebrews 12:2). I believe He was buoyed up by the knowledge of what He was achieving on the cross. Jesus knew that the reason He had come into this world was to undo the works of the devil. He knew that on the cross He was achieving a total, once-for-all victory for mankind over all the evil in the world. He knew that on the third day He would rise again from the grave, having now overcome death, and that some six weeks later He would be entering into His glory, and would be seated at His Father's right hand in heaven.

Here I believe we have the real message of the cross. I have always questioned whether there was any merit in suffering *for its own sake*. The message of the cross is victory. We are told of Jesus' last great cry from the cross which has often been translated, 'It is accomplished!' In today's language I think the words which Jesus shouted would have been, 'I've done it! I've won!'

Jesus was in control to the very end. After He had let out this great shout none of the four Gospels tells us that He 'died'. Two of them recount that Jesus 'breathed his last', whilst the other two make it more specific and tell us that Jesus 'gave up his spirit'. Even His passing from life in this world was a deliberate act on His part.

Nowadays if someone dies the law requires a medical certificate signed by a doctor giving the cause of death. If such a certificate had been required 2000 years ago, bearing in mind John's evidence about the water and the blood which spurted out when His side was pierced (John 19:34), we can be fairly sure that the cause of death would have been entered as 'cardiac rupture'. In plain language, if a person dies from cardiac rupture it means they die of a broken heart.

CHAPTER 39

# The Victory of the Cross

I remember a man who had previously been a Satanist telling me they had been taught that in the end Satan 'got' Jesus when he had Him on the cross, and that there he killed off Jesus.

I mention this only to emphasise how diametrically opposite the truth is. The fundamental message of the cross is that Jesus who died, and rose again, broke the power of Satan once and for all as He shed His blood on the cross.

John writes that Jesus said, '"It is finished." With that, he bowed his head and gave up his spirit' (John 19:30). The words He used were the words that were written on a bill when it had been paid. At that moment He knew that He had paid the price for the sins of mankind. It was a tremendous cry of victory over all the powers of darkness.

I often find myself saying to people who come to the Mission, 'If it is true – as it is – that Jesus broke Satan's power on the cross, once and for all, and if you, yourself, have truly accepted Jesus as your Saviour and your Lord, then with Jesus you can't help winning!' In racing terms, you are backing the winner.

Many of us are conscious of being involved in spiritual warfare. Many of us are conscious that Satan seems to be throwing everything at us, to try and get us down. It is at those moments that we need to come back to fundamentals. Jesus won on the cross and if He is our Lord and Saviour, then with Him we can win over anything that comes to us from Satan.

When Paul wrote to the Ephesians, he wanted them to know Jesus' 'incomparably great power for us who believe'. He went on: 'That power is like the working of [God's] mighty strength, which he exerted in Christ when he raised him from the dead and seated him at his right hand in the heavenly realms' (Ephesians 1:19–20). Think of having within you that same mighty power which actually raised Jesus from the dead!

The world says that 'seeing is believing'. Not surprisingly things are the other way round – the right way round – for the Christian. For us believing is seeing. When Jesus called Peter from over the water I don't think Peter questioned whether, when he got out of the boat, the water would actually support him. He didn't know that he had within him the faith to give his feet firm footholds on the turbulent surface of the sea. But he stepped on to the water and it did support him.

In the same way we won't know the power of the risen Christ which we have within us until we use it! It is only as we use it that we realise His tremendous power.

Paul wrote to Timothy that in the last days people will have a form of godliness but denying its power (2 Timothy 3:5). How true this is of so many of us today! Until the power comes back into the body of Christ, His church, the great majority of people in this country will continue to think of Christianity as nothing more than a harmless relic of a bygone age. Paul wrote, 'The kingdom of God is not a matter of talk but of power' (1 Corinthians 4:20).

Let us resolve to use the power that is in the name of Jesus, in the cross of Jesus and in His blood, and let us resolve to go forth victorious with Jesus into the spiritual warfare into which we've been called.

CHAPTER 40

# The Motorway

Imagine you are driving along a motorway. You've driven quite a long way and you decide that a cup of coffee would be welcome. So, at the next service station, you pull in, park your car, and climb the steps to the cafeteria.

You collect your coffee and look round to see if there is a free table, but the place is quite full. There is one table with only one person sitting there. 'Do you mind if I sit at your table?' you ask. In reply you get a wave to the empty chair. Of course, you discuss the weather. But there comes a time when even the English weather ceases to be interesting!

'Where are you driving to?' you then politely ask your table companion. Imagine your surprise when the person replies, 'I don't know!'

A thought occurs to you. 'Perhaps you're not driving along the motorway at all?' you ask. 'I expect you live locally and have just dropped into the cafeteria here for a morning cup of coffee?'

'No,' the answer comes back, 'I have been driving along the motorway.'

This reply leaves you more puzzled than ever. Then a possible explanation dawns on you.

'Perhaps you are driving along the motorway for fun, and because you enjoy the driving?' you ask.

'No,' the person replies, 'I'm driving along the motorway, but I don't know where I'm going and, if I ask myself, I don't really get much enjoyment out of it.'

This story is, of course, imaginary. But it is a true description of the lives of many Christians! Many Christians wander, rather aimlessly, through life, not getting any particular enjoyment out of it, and not really knowing where they are going.

Paul wrote: 'For to me, to live is Christ and to die is gain' (Philippians 1:21). I don't believe that this life makes sense unless one sees it in the context of eternity. The key question is this: Do we believe in our hearts that our ultimate destination is heaven?

We need to remember the 'hope' that Paul wrote about (e.g., Colossians 1:27). He was thinking of the hope of glory which is to be ours for ever. When we are feeling oppressed there is such wonderful reassurance for us as we remember that God reigns in His heaven and that, in the fullness of time, we shall be going there to join Him in everlasting joy and bliss. It is then that we are strengthened, as we reaffirm that the same God is in control of this world, that He is perfect love and that we can trust Him completely.

We do well at times to contemplate what it will be like when eventually we are in the direct presence of God Himself, no longer seeing through a glass darkly, but face to face (1 Corinthians 13:12, AV). Imagine if one of us in our present state of sinfulness were to come into the presence of the awesome holiness of God! Imagine what it would be like to be face to face with the absolute righteousness and the utter holiness of God Himself. I know what my reaction would be. In horror I would cry out, 'Lord, spare me! I can't take it! It is too wonderful and I just can't bear it!'

This was Isaiah's reaction: 'Woe to me!' he cried. 'I am ruined! For I am a man of unclean lips, and I live among a people of unclean lips, and my eyes have seen the King, the LORD Almighty!' (Isaiah 6:5). You will remember God had to send one of the seraphim with a burning coal to cleanse his lips.

Habakkuk tells us the reason: God cannot look on sin (Habakkuk 1:13). I believe this is because His holiness is so staggering that if any sin were somehow to come into His direct presence it would simply shrivel up and cease to exist.

When God made the world, it must have been perfect. How could a God who is Himself perfect have deliberately created a world which was as imperfect as the world we see around us today? This view seems to be borne out in Genesis 1 where the words are repeated several times, 'God saw that it was good', and then, 'God saw all that he had made, and it was very good' (Genesis 1:31).

We often forget how desperately disappointed God must have been when mankind turned against Him at the fall. Indeed, as I dictate this, the word 'disappointed' seems far too weak a word; perhaps we are closer to the truth if I suggest that God must have been devastated at the time of the fall. He had made the world to be a perfect dwelling place for mankind, and now mankind had turned their backs on Him and had spoiled all His wonderful work – yet He still wants to have us working with Him in His task (see 1 Corinthians 3:9 and 2 Corinthians 6:1).

If God had been less than perfect, He would have written the whole of creation off, there and then. But the patience and, indeed, the sheer humility of God continually amazes me. He kept on with His work in this world, but ever since the fall His longing must have been for us to turn back to Him and allow Him to make perfect that which He originally created to be perfect, namely, all creation including mankind.

I believe that when the time comes for the gates of heaven to be thrown open for us and when, to the singing of angels, we are ushered into the direct presence of God, we will be changed by then into His likeness. Jesus told us, 'Be perfect' and in case we hadn't taken that in, He added, 'as your heavenly Father is perfect' (Matthew 5:48). Similarly, Peter quotes God in the Old Testament as saying, 'Be holy, because I am holy' (1 Peter 1:16). In Peter's second letter he says that we ourselves will actually share in the divine nature of God (2 Peter 1:4).

I believe that our entire life in this world is simply a preparation for heaven. I don't believe that one can make sense of this life unless one sees it in the context of eternity.

I believe that in this life God begins the process of making us sinless and perfect and preparing us for the indescribable joy of spending all eternity with Him in heaven. But life is far too short for God to complete His work in this world.

I believe the work is completed after death, and we are given a clue as to how this will come about when Paul writes that, at some point after we die, 'we will all be changed ... in the twinkling of an eye' (1 Corinthians 15:51–52).

Paul wrote, 'If only for this life we have hope ... we are to be pitied more than all men' (1 Corinthians 15:19). I believe we need to keep reminding ourselves of the unbelievable glory which will be ours in heaven, and that the purpose of this life is for God to start getting us ready for the moment when we ourselves are ushered in through heaven's gates.

But if heaven is our destination, how are we going to get there? What is abundantly clear is that none of us is capable of making himself or herself perfect and thus able to 'qualify' for entry into heaven.

Mankind upset God's perfect plan by rebelling against Him, as represented in the story of the fall. Ever since then, as we have seen, the longing in the heart of God must have been for Him to make perfect once again His creation in each one of us. But He has given us free will and He always respects our free will. He waits for us to turn to Him – humbling ourselves before Him, seeking to discern what He is longing to do in us, and in those around us, and then praying in line with His perfect will (1 John 5:14). That is the prayer which releases the power of God to work in us and to work through us.

Healing is the process of God gradually perfecting His work in us, and the power to heal lies in the dynamic relationship of love between us and God, He in us, each loving the other, and each receiving the other's love.

It was in His victory on the cross that Jesus broke the hold of evil over mankind, and it is the blood of Jesus, shed for us on the cross, which the powers of darkness simply cannot stand.

But we need to avail ourselves of His victory which He won for us and to step out and start using the power which so often is lying latent within us. Each one of us who has been baptised in the name of the Trinity has the power of the Holy Spirit dwelling within, but we need to use that power. We won't know that we've got it until we first step out and use it.

It is as we move on with Jesus in this life that we realise that imperceptibly, and gradually, He is changing us and that the process of changing us is rooted in our relationship of love with Him. We need to acknowledge and, indeed, praise Him that He loves us. We need continually to reaffirm our love for Him and we need that divine dissatisfaction with ourselves which causes us continually to reach out for more and more of Jesus.

There will be trials on the way. Until we commit ourselves to Jesus, Satan doesn't bother too much about us as, until then, we present no threat to him. But once we have become Christians, the going often becomes harder, for Satan will now be getting scared and he will throw everything at us.

But as we hold on to Jesus and seek to draw closer and closer to Him, we find that in the end God 'uses' Satan. In all things God works for good for those who love Him (Romans 8:28) and as, holding on to Jesus, we triumph in the tribulations which come our way, so we grow stronger in

Jesus and through all the tribulations we experience the wonderful inner joy which He alone can give us.

Sadly, there are many Christians in our churches today who are, as it were, travelling along the motorway not knowing where they're going and not particularly enjoying the travelling. Let us be clear in our own minds about the wonderful glory which lies ahead for us. Let us experience the joy of the Lord as we proceed on our way with Him, and, as we grow in His love, let us satisfy our inner longing and reach out continually for more and more of Jesus.